PROSPERITY
*or*STUPIDITY

The Choice Is Ours

David D. Lowry

ISBN: 1-4781-7911-2

ISBN-13: 9781478179115

Library of Congress Control Number: 2012912034

CreateSpace Independent Publishing Platform

North Charleston, South Carolina

Democracy is the worst form of government, except for all the others that have been tried from time to time.

— Winston Churchill

Democracy is a device that ensures we shall be governed no better than we deserve.

— George Bernard Shaw

To Loni,
my dear wife and extraordinary partner

Contents

Introduction

Happiness is a state of mind that does not depend on what we have. While that's true enough, prosperity gives us more opportunities to pursue happiness. We generally think of prosperity as having enough money for a comfortable life free of financial concerns and the means and time to enjoy life the way we want to. The other part of prosperity is having the freedom to pursue happiness as we wish.

It is strange that, while virtually everyone wants prosperity, we so often do things as a nation to impede achieving it. This occurs when we make emotionally based decisions and adopt policies that provide near-term gratification at the expense of longer term planning that would ultimately produce far more benefit. Much of government action amounts to "eating our seed corn."

This is the unfortunate victory of emotion over common sense. Most people have an innate understanding of the fundamental truths of life. But unfortunately, we often succumb to acting on wishes of how we want things to be rather than on how the world really is. For example, we know intuitively that we can't get something for nothing, but we are prone to act as though we can.

Most nations are replete with policies and programs that demonstrate this. Basically these are government "services" that take from one group to provide benefits to another group. While it is beneficial and even necessary to do this to a reasonable degree to promote the growth of a nation's prosperity, the destructive results of excessive redistribution and deficit spending are conveniently overlooked by many.

1 Prosperity Versus Stupidity

It is stupid to act in ways that are contrary to the laws of nature—to do things based on how we wish the world worked rather than the way it actually does work and then expect a positive outcome. Imagine what would happen if we tried to send a rocket to the moon but ignored basic laws of physics and chemistry. For example, if instead of using regular rocket fuel we filled the rocket's tanks with chicken soup because we wanted the soup to work as fuel in order to save money. This would obviously be crazy.

Yet it is amazing how the United States and most other countries routinely defy common sense and ignore other basic laws of how the world works when it comes to their policies and how a country is run. Many basic rules are incredibly simple:

- *We can't get something for nothing.*
- *We can't consume more than we produce without taking it from someone else or borrowing against the future.*

- *We won't do or produce anything unless we are motivated by the expectation of reward.*
- *No one has a right to do or take anything that violates someone else's rights.*
- *Nature does not treat everyone the same in what they get in life. Systems that strive for economic equality fail because they violate one or more of the above principles.*

The consequences of ignoring these and other fundamental truths are generally not felt as quickly as ignoring a physical law, like stepping off a cliff. But to the extent that we follow the stupidity of wishful thinking that is inconsistent with how things actually work, we compromise the prosperity and quality of life within a country. Accordingly, the way to greater prosperity is to examine issues logically and agree on the best ways to get there. As things stand now, we are operating in ways that are self-destructive, even to those who are the primary beneficiaries of the deficit spending, the "social safety net," subsidies, special tax breaks, and other forms of government largesse.

America has another problem that goes beyond policies based on unrealistic ideas. Namely, far-left movements that got their foothold in the 1930s during the crisis of the Great Depression and have gained traction ever since. The result has been the steady growth of wealth redistribution, government regulation, and the erosion of our Constitution and personal freedom. This has been a deliberate effort by factions within the United States to move the country toward becoming a socialistic welfare state. And some have endeavored to go even further, wanting to make the United States into a worker's utopia along the lines of Communism.

As Saul Alinsky, one of the extreme proponents of such a revolution, put it in describing one of his books: "*The Prince* was written by Machiavelli for the Haves on how to hold power. [My book] *Rules for Radicals* is written for the Have-Nots on how to take it away."

2 The Land of 'Fair Share'

Once there was a country that developed a high level of social consciousness based on the idea that everyone should pay their "fair share" and receive their "fair share."

It became generally understood that each person is born with certain abilities or disabilities, and with dispositions to strive or not to strive. Each person is born into different circumstances; he or she may live in a family with financial well-being or poverty, and may have supportive or harmful parents, in a place of much or little opportunity. Added to this are all of a person's experiences, good luck and bad luck, successes and failures. In short, what a person is and has at every point in life is the result of how fortunate they have been. Simply put, what a person has is due to luck.

Some might disagree saying that successful people have applied themselves, worked hard, made good choices and have been responsible, to which the response was, "True, but it was their good fortune to have, or be influenced to have, these attributes."

Accordingly, the notion developed over time that some people were simply luckier than others were, and therefore in fairness there should be a redistribution of wealth so that everyone could enjoy about the same standard of living. This was considered social justice by many. Namely, "From each according to his ability, to each according to his need." (Karl Marx).

The Land of Fair Share had an effective government that provided for the safety of its people, law and order, the smooth operation of commerce and operation of society. Of course, all of this took money, which called for taxation. Initially, the government was primarily funded through excise taxes, and this provided more than enough money except in time of war. But some people thought this was not fair since it amounted to an imputed tax on what people buy. Because the poor spend all of their money and the rich do not, the wealthy pay a smaller percentage tax on their total income.

Now it is logical to contend that each person receives about the same amount of benefit from government activities so everyone should pay the *same dollar amount* for it. It's like going to a store where everyone pays the same amount for the same item. But this logic was lost on social engineers of the time, and so an income tax was introduced.

Based on the reasoning of the income tax promoters, one would think the fair thing to do would be to tax everyone's income at the same rate. But no, they went the next step, and decided that the higher one's income, the higher the tax rate should be. It started out as a 2 percent tax on incomes over $4,000, which would be an income of $90,800 today. This income level was so high that it affected only 1 percent of the households at the time, so naturally the income tax was a popular idea. The highest tax rate was 7 percent on income that would now be $11,360,000 plus there were lots of ways of avoiding much of the tax.

This was the country's initial flirtation with income redistribution. It didn't seem too onerous at the start, but that would change. As time went on, politicians continued to curry favor with their constituents by expanding the services of government. They could take pride in this noble work even though it was with other people's money.

And the monster started to grow. The initial income tax law was fourteen pages long, but over the next ninety-nine years, it grew to a gargantuan 75,000 pages, including associated regulations, rulings, and other pertinent material. The tax code was subject to constant tinkering as political winds shifted back and forth, and government used the tax system to favor various policies and constituencies. During wartime, rates went up dramatically, but afterward tax rates would come down more slowly and sometimes not at all.

Eventually about half of the population was paying no income tax at all, and some were even being given money to supplement their income. At this point, the wealthiest 10 percent of the people were paying 70 percent of the federal income tax, not to mention business taxes, property taxes, death taxes, sales taxes, and many more. Even so, wealthier people were accused of not paying their fair share. Interestingly, no one was asking if people who were paying no income tax at all were paying their share of the fare.

Through the years the country prospered based on a culture and environment that offered the opportunity for success to those who applied themselves. People were motivated by the notion that they should keep and enjoy what they earn. Unfortunately, there was a growing opinion that in fairness the government should provide ever-increasing benefits to the less successful at the expense of the more successful.

The country had evolved into two groups: those that produced more than they consumed (Producers) and those that consumed more than they produced (Takers). So it came to pass that the country reached a tipping point.

The Takers and the idealists who promoted the justice of economic equality became the controlling majority in the country. Under the mantra that those that are most financially successful must pay their "fair share," the burden of paying the country's bills was placed ever more heavily on the Producers.

Often new programs and entitlements were created in the name of providing an ever-increasing social safety net. The programs were typically implemented without consideration for the impact of unfunded mandates or the burdens they would place on business, individuals, states, the economy, or the ability to compete in the world.

In this process the government grew and became increasingly expensive. So much money was needed that taxes alone could not pay the bill. So the government borrowed and printed vast amounts of money. This made the people's money worth less as it became stealthily devalued. The interest the country had to pay on its national debt became enormous, adding dramatically to the cost of government. Unfortunately, a very large part of the voting population did not understand or pay attention to these issues. They thought that they could continue to get ever more from the government by simply increasing the taxes on millionaires and billionaires. After all, these rich people had more money than they needed or could even spend.

The fact that this "extra" money was either invested or became available for others to borrow was ignored. And the reality that these uses helped to drive an economy, and create jobs and other income opportunities was conveniently overlooked.

What the blind idealists and Takers did not realize were the ultimate consequences of a Robin Hood-inspired "take from the rich and give to the poor" society. Remember that we are influenced by what we learn along our path. If we observe that we will fare adequately even if we drop out of school or do poorly, do not strive for achievement, and are protected from folly and failure, then why make the effort? If we take responsibility, work hard, save, invest, take risks, strive for success, but too much is taken from us, then why make the effort? Why not pack up and leave or simply stop saving, working, making investments, or taking the risk to start a new business? (The aroma of cooked goose started to fill the air.)

So as the flag of Fair Share continued to wave, the population of Takers grew ever larger, and the number of Producers diminished until there was no one left to produce. The country could no longer pay for the interest on its debt, let alone pay back its debt. So understandably no one would lend it any more money. The Fairsharians resorted to printing more and more money, which became increasingly worthless. This made it even less attractive to lend to or invest in the country. Finally the country tried to respond by cutting back on benefits, but the population was addicted. Riots and disorder ensued as the population demanded the continuation of "their fix" of unfunded goodies. So the land of Fair Share went sliding down the slope of national decline.

The goose of incentive and entrepreneurial capitalism that had laid the golden eggs was dead on its back, in a ditch with its feet pointing skyward. People in their misery would walk by and spit on it for having failed them so badly. After all, their sad state was not their fault. To them the blame rested on the failure of their leaders, ignoring the fact that the people had chosen them, and on stingy rich people who did not want to give up most of what they earned.

They did not appreciate that the goose would no longer give a hoot when its life became too taxing.

3 Self-Interest

Self-interest is often confused with selfishness. Self-interest is actually a good thing, as it enables us to survive and prosper. In fact we all have self-interest, along with every other creature on the planet. If there were ever creatures that did not have an interest in their own well-being, they would have died out quickly when they became a predator's meal ticket or had to compete for scarce resources.

There is **Sociopathic Self-Interest** in which a person is self-serving by exploiting and preying on others and society in general. This type of person either has no sense of interpersonal ethics or chooses to ignore the rights of others to gain personal advantage.

With **Exploitive Self-Interest** one seeks to dominate others in order to gain power. With this power the person seeks to impose his or her ideas and beliefs on others in order to achieve various objectives such as the promulgation of a political/economic system, social standards, or religious beliefs. The power may also be used to obtain wealth, ego gratification, and other benefits. Often exploitive self-interest is based on one's egocentric notion that he or she "knows what is right" and sees any machinations as justified and noble. Exploitive self-interest uses fear, deception, manipulation, and force to achieve its ends. This is distinct from the effort to influence others by sharing of ideas, opinions, and information without the use of psychological, economic, or physical coercion.

There are many people who have **Blind Self-Interest** and seek to take from others through a third party—namely government. While these people would not steal directly from another person, they are blind (by choice or ignorance) to the fact that the government is doing the stealing for them. Of course this redistribution of assets is done in good conscience and even with a sense of righteousness as it is carried out in the name of social justice.

A person with **Passive Self-Interest** lives his or her life and pursues happiness while respecting the rights of others and following the rules and norms of the society in which he or she lives.

With **Enlightened Self-Interest**, a person seeks his or her well-being and enjoyment while understanding that contributing to others enhances his or her life and the lives of others. It is the social evolution from which we are humanitarian, cooperative, and work together to achieve more than we can alone.

It is a fundamental truth that everyone acts in their self-interest even when doing selfless acts. When we do things that are selfless, we have a sense of satisfaction that comes from living according to our personal values. It is folly to proceed on a course of action on the supposition that any group of people will be motivated by something other than their self-interest.

Even in communal groups such as nuns and monks, each individual is pursuing their own self-interest based on their beliefs and other motivations, even though the participants are highly cooperative to the point of significant self-denial. It should also be noted that in small communal societies, members are there by choice or birth. But people in a larger society resist communal dictates; typically they want none of it.

4 The Failure to Allow Failure

Competition is the engine of improvement. It is the way in which alternatives are tested and compared. Those that are most successful are kept, and the losers are discarded. This is the natural selection process that applies not only to biological evolution but also to the improvement of almost everything, including social structures, products, business practices, forms of government, athletes, and so on.

Without competition and the opportunity for success and failure, ongoing improvement stagnates. Unfortunately, there is a growing trend to protect people and institutions from failure. Here are some examples:

- *The government gives or lends money to a company to keep it from going out of business. This perpetuates poor management, products that are outdated or otherwise inferior, and businesses that are no longer competitive and have less-efficient means of production. This is done using tax revenue paid by more successful companies and the population at large. Thus other* companies have less money to use, and people have less discretionary income to enjoy.

- A school decides that their standard grading system is hurtful to students who get low grades. Accordingly they implement a pass/fail system or simply pass everyone to the next grade regardless of their performance. Of course this takes away incentive to attend class, do homework, and study except for a few students who are exceptionally motivated.

- People in government, education, and union shops have work rules or regulations that prevent them from being fired even if their work is substandard. This, of course, robs employment from others who could do the job better, and it cheats students and others who receive the shoddy services or work. Once again, those who are energetic, responsible, and productive subsidize those who are not. In addition, unions often hamper organizations from becoming more efficient and effective.

- In Communist East Germany, it made little difference whether a person showed up for work or did a good job. No one ever got fired, and getting ahead was based on a person's connections. Productivity there, as well in Communist countries in general, was abysmal as was the standard of living. In contrast, a place like Singapore only provides a place for a person to live. Other than *that, a person has to work if they want to eat. Singapore has high productivity and a correspondingly good standard of living. (The country is a bit anal in that it fines people for failing to flush a public toilet, but it is still a good place to get ahead.)*

One of the attributes that contributes greatly to people's happiness is an attitude of taking personal responsibility. They take responsibility for taking care of their health, for using opportunity to become educated, doing good work, caring for their families, being considerate, being a good citizen, earning a living, and handling the consequences of their mistakes.

We learn the value of being responsible from our life experiences. However, if we are protected from the consequences of being irresponsible then we fail to learn to be responsible. That is why government programs that save us from our mistakes are particularly harmful.

If we cause a problem to our health due to smoking, excessive drug use, dangerous activities, and other potentially damaging pursuits, then we should not expect others to pay for the consequences. If we don't apply ourselves in learning and don't develop skills that justify the level of earnings we want, why should we be guaranteed a higher wage? If we make bad investments or run a business that results in loss, why should we be bailed out at the expense of others?

This is not to say there shouldn't be K-12 education and some level of a safety net for children, assistance for those who are truly in need, or clinic-level basic health care for adults. But to create a plush cradle of freebees for an entire population is not only unaffordable but also creates dependency and destroys incentive to be responsible.

A country will prosper only if its people take personal responsibility for the betterment of themselves, their communities, and their country. This will not happen if its businesses, institutions, or people are overly protected from failure.

Failure is nature's secret sauce for sorting out that which works best and thereby improving the world. Ironically, to prevent failure is ultimately to invite it.

5 The Drip, Drip, Drip of Freedom Seeping Away

There is a useful level of regulation that is beneficial and even essential for a well functioning society. For example, if there were not traffic laws, driving would be extremely dangerous and chaotic; if there weren't environmental laws there would be serious pollution. However, the amount of regulation needs to be balanced between its cost and its benefits. Traffic deaths from driving could be reduced dramatically if the maximum speed limit was twenty miles per hour, but the costs resulting from our limited mobility would be draconian.

It is appealing when government sets out to protect us from failure and adversity. However, the comfy nest of protection comes at a high price when regulation is excessive. In freeing us from taking responsibility for our mistakes and their consequences, government simultaneously limits what we are allowed to do. We trade our freedom for security.

What is even worse, the limits are usually extensive enough to protect even the most inept and irresponsible people. So for those who are prudent, sensible, and responsible, the amount of freedom lost is disproportionately high relative to the benefit received. And often the "protections" have consequences that are worse than the problem they are aimed at. Here are a few:

"Protection"	Unintended Consequences
Consumer Protection	*Law suits make a few people rich, but drive up prices for all consumers.*
Malpractice Lawsuits	*Unlimited damage awards have led to extremely high malpractice insurance costs for doctors adding significantly to the cost of medical care.*
HIPPA	*Excessive privacy protections add substantial additional work for health care providers adding to medical costs.*
Land Use Restrictions	*Overregulation impedes desirable development. At times the resulting devaluation in land holdings robs value from businesses and individuals.*
Controlled Substances	*Excessive and unwarranted regulations increase costs, promote organized crime, put thousands in jail, lead to huge enforcement costs and interfere with freedom to enjoy what we want to.*
EPA	*Overregulation impedes business and imposes major costs on industries.*

Endangered Species	*The ESA is used to halt industrial and recreational development often with severe economic consequences. It puts protecting some inconsequential organisms over human welfare.*
OSHA	*Over-enforcement imposes requirements and penalties on businesses for things that have little actual impact on worker safety.*

The laws and regulations that put these protections in place usually fail to consider their economic impact and the effect they will have on the ability of United States companies to compete in international markets. There are attorneys who love these regulations and become wealthy pursuing high-dollar lawsuits that these "protections" spawn.

Environmental groups often abuse federal regulations by filing endless lawsuits to promote their often-narrow agendas at the cost to larger society of lost jobs, lost recreational opportunities, negative economic consequences, and greatly increased time and expense for worthwhile projects. We should be bugged if protecting an insignificant insect takes precedence over the well-being of people.

Judging by the wealth of unintended consequences that arise from the laws and programs enacted by politicians, it is clear that many legislators would be poor at playing pool or chess, where thinking several steps ahead is essential. Politicians are compelled to show that they are doing something, so they enact laws they believe will be popular with their constituents.

The result is an ever-growing mountain of laws that create a menacing jungle for people, businesses, and other organizations to navigate. And lurking in that jungle is the feasting monstrosity of big government. Its insatiable appetite for our wealth and the fruits of our labor is fed by elected leaders who dole out from a trough that is continually filled through endless borrowing. This creature is ever more intrusive in our lives as it bites off chunks of our freedom at every opportunity. It insidiously creeps up on us as it soothingly says, "I am here to take care of you and provide for your safety. Don't worry about failing because I won't let it happen. I will take responsibility for your well-being. You needn't bother. Trust me."

6 The Right Stuff

The Declaration of Independence makes a general statement about our rights as human beings. The following is an interpretation that should help to clarify the intent of the original words.

We hold these truths to be self-evident

That all men are created equal

(We all have the same rights.)

That they are endowed by their Creator

(Rights that we have by birth.)

With certain unalienable Rights

(Rights that cannot be take from us.)

That Among these Rights

(These aren't the only rights.)

Are Life

(The right to live,)

Liberty

(The right to do as we please,)

And the pursuit of happiness.

(The right to seek happiness as we wish.)

Of course this also means that in exercising our rights we must not impose on or diminish the rights of others.

Some people contend that these rights are the result of agreement of our founding fathers and are not inherent to all humans. While there may have been debate at one time, freedom that is "life, liberty, and the pursuit of happiness" is a fundamental right of every person, even though this was not recognized until recent times.

Throughout most of history, kings, emperors, chiefs, and other rulers claimed rights over everyone else, and the rights of individuals were only those granted by higher authority. It was convenient for monarchs to declare that they had "divine rights" that were theirs exclusively. This was a generally accepted convention throughout most of human history, but it was a belief not supported by the truth.

Let's take a look. Assume that there is only one person on earth. That person would be free to do anything he or she wished. Now assume there are just two people on earth. There is simply no natural-law reason for one person to have more freedom than another. If one or more people come up with criteria that give one person or group greater freedom than others, the criteria would obviously be based on subjective opinion, and as such has no claim to being objective truth.

If there is competition for resources, there may be conflict resulting in a winner and a loser. But this behavior does not change the fact that each person has an equal natural right to be free. "Might makes right" is nothing more than the self-serving opinion of those with power.

There is considerable confusion about what are rights of ours, and things that are not rights but rather services provided by the government.

The US Constitution enumerates certain rights specifically:

- *The right to move about as we wish*
- *The right to practice the religion of our choice*
- *The right to speak freely*
- *The right to a free press*
- *The right to assemble*
- *The right to be free of unreasonable searches and seizures*
- *The right to own property*
- *The right to compensation if our property is taken*
- *The right to vote*
- *The right to own and use arms*
- *The right to due process if charged with a crime*
- *The right to the presumption of innocence*
- *The right to be confronted by an accuser*
- *The right to be free of discrimination*

Notice that these are rights to be free, to make our own choices, to determine how and by whom we are governed, and to enjoy our material possessions and dispose of them as we choose. In short, to pursue happiness as we choose. On the other hand, the following are not rights. And in fact they usually diminish the freedom of one group to benefit another group. If someone gets something he or she didn't pay for, then it comes at a cost to someone else.

We do not have an innate or constitutional right to:

- *Health care*
- *Insurance*
- *Education*
- *Housing*
- *A job*
- *Welfare*
- *A minimum wage*
- *A living wage*
- *Preferential treatment*
- *Supplemental income*

However, these things are often claimed as rights by those who want other citizens to pay for the benefits government gives to them. Recently "women's health" has been touted as a right, even to the extent of infringing on our constitutional right to religious freedom. On this basis, the federal government is mandating that birth control, sterilization, and pill-induced abortion be provided to employees via their insurance plans even if the employer has a religious objection.

In so doing, the Congress and the administration are not only inventing a new right but are also promulgating it in violation of the Constitution. Furthermore, contending that women have a right that goes beyond the rights of men is also blatantly inconsistent with the Constitution.

To be clear, under the Constitution new rights can only be established by an amendment, which follows a very specific process. It requires a two-thirds vote by both houses of Congress and ratification by three-fourths of the states. Neither the legislative nor executive branches of government can proclaim a new right, regardless of how beneficial it might appear to be. In fact the president has no role whatever in the amendment process.

Accordingly, the items listed above are *benefits* not rights. These benefits are provided when a society judges that it is in its best interest to do so. The question is, how much should the Producers contribute to provide these benefits to the Takers? What is the optimum balance between the positive consequences of providing benefits and taking more than an equitable amount from the Producers?

It bears repeating.

We don't have a right to anything for free, because if we get something for free, someone else has to pay for it, which violates their right to their own possessions.

As the saying goes, "It is unjust to rob Peter to pay Paul." However, even though free services are not a right, it is beneficial to society to provide *reasonable levels* of security, education, health care, food, and so forth, to promote productivity and to be humanitarian. This is a basic justification for unequal taxation.

Naturally, the Takers will consider generous government programs to be "reasonable" since it is their way of getting more without having to pay for it. So it is not surprising that as Takers get more power as their numbers grow, government and benefits increase. Originally only male land owners could vote in national elections. They were predominately the best educated and productive of their day. Over time this has changed; the less productive and less educated are becoming the predominant voting bloc. In effect, a system of legalized stealing through the voting process emerges. This is not only an egregious violation of human rights, but it ultimately threatens the ongoing viability of democracy.

The Bill of Rights guarantees our right to own property, and to be fairly compensated if it is taken for a public purpose. Unfortunately, there are extensive abuses by all levels of government when it places restrictions on land that reduce its value but pays no compensation. This theft is often justified by the notion that the government doesn't have the money to pay the property owner, so this somehow gives government the right simply to take it. This, in fact, is saying it's okay to violate an individual's rights for the sake of convenience.

There is an insidious notion that just because an individual has substantially more wealth than the average person that they have an obligation to pay a far greater portion of what they have into the public treasury. This is a violation of the right of an individual to own and enjoy their possessions. Our founding fathers understood that if we don't respect the rights of the individual, in time the rights of everyone erode. In the school of sound economics, Socialists get poor Marx.

In 1513, Niccolo Machiavelli published *The Prince*, in which he espoused the philosophy "the end justifies the means." This means that it is okay to do anything in order to achieve a desired result. For example, the rights of one person or group can be violated for the benefit of another. According to this thinking, it is okay for the government to give preference to a particular group in educational enrollment, hiring, or contracting based on sex or race.

7 Truth Versus Demagoguery

It is common for people to use catch phrases to justify what they want when it is not supported by reason. We will examine a few of them, including "fair share," "social justice," "living wage," the right to education, health care, welfare, and so forth.

The truth is:

Each person's "fair share" is what he or she has, and it doesn't include something that belongs to someone else.

Fair Share: A person's *fair share contribution* to government is about the same amount for everyone based on the premise that everyone receives about the same level of benefit from the government. However, for practical reasons lower-income people contribute less than their fair share, and higher-income people give more than their fair share.

Flat Tax: A true *flat tax* is one in which everyone pays the same amount for what they receive. A *flat percentage tax* is one in which everyone pays the same percentage of their income.

Social Justice: Social justice is where everyone has the freedom to live and act however they wish as long as they don't interfere with the rights and freedom of others.

Poverty Level: Benchmarks such as poverty level and living wage are subjective and arbitrary, and they are used to justify income redistribution programs.

The right to...: As we have already seen, under the Constitution, no one has a right to a social service such as education, health care, supplemental income, and so forth. There is no such thing as special rights for women, men, or minorities. It is ironic that some groups that cried out loudest for equal rights now want to enjoy rights that are superior to the rights of others.

Income Gap: The income gap between low and high income earners is used liberally to argue for increasing taxes on the wealthy, especially if the gap is increasing. But this is an illogical argument. The real question should be whether the lower-income people have the exercise of their constitutional rights and reasonable support from society and a decent living, provided an individual is willing to apply himself or herself. There is absolutely no guarantee or right to any level of income parity as an endowment by our creator as stated in the Declaration of Independence. Already the top half of the country's earners pays virtually all of the national income tax. So it is absurd to argue that, as a matter of equity, they should pay more.

Social Security Tax: It is said that the 45 percent of people in the United States who do not pay any federal income tax do pay Social Security and Medicare "taxes." The reality is that these people don't pay any federal tax because these "taxes" are actually payments into retirement income and medical services plans.

A country enters a national death spiral when a majority of its voting population demands so much that to pay its bills government prints money wildly, borrows lavishly, and hamstrings or drives away its Producers with excessive taxation and regulation.

The problem with a "nanny state" is that it becomes a single-parent family with no breadwinner.

8 Reason Rules

Any government that operates with disregard for how the world works and ignores the laws of basic economics will fail in time. The country will be at a competitive disadvantage with others, quality of life will erode, and ultimately people will revolt.

A society that does not understand how human motivation works is inefficient, and productivity declines. Its people and politicians are delusional as they ignore reality in preference to their beliefs and dreams of how they want the world to work. Due to unrealistic idealism, errant ideology, narrow self-interest, or ignorance, people, and politicians operate contrary to the laws of nature. They are like a person who skydives without a parachute believing he or she can fly.

It is reason that enables us to understand how our world works physically, individually, socially, and economically. The more we know about how things work and act in accord with that knowledge, the more likely we are to succeed.

So here are a few fundamental laws of economics that are self-evident and govern the material quality of our lives.

A people cannot consume more than they produce, at least not indefinitely.

Production is the result of constructive human action.

People are productive only if there is adequate incentive to be so.

Could anything be more obvious? It is stunning to see the vast number of people who either don't know or ignore these basic principles.

Productivity

There are a number of elements that contribute to productivity:

- **Work:** *Investment of time and effort.*
- **Capital:** *Investment of money and other resources.*
- **Risk:** *Willingness to take risks for future rewards.*
- **Ability:** *Education, health, belief in oneself, optimism, drive.*
- **Tools:** *Machinery, access to information, resources.*

- **Forms of organization:** *Types of businesses that allow for organized effort.*
- **Supportive environment:** *Markets for goods, services and skills, courts and sound laws, sources of capital, banking system, good infrastructure, safe and stable environment, protection for creative works.*

The element of investment involves taking the risk that, by forgoing immediate gratification of spending and relaxing now, there will be a greater future return. If the prospect of greater future enjoyment is not great enough, or the likelihood of achieving it is not high enough, people will not invest themselves and their resources.

Incentive

There are a lot of things that motivate us, like money, which can be used to obtain so many things. But beyond money we seek to fill a wide range of needs. A good depiction of this is Maslow's Hierarchy of Needs.

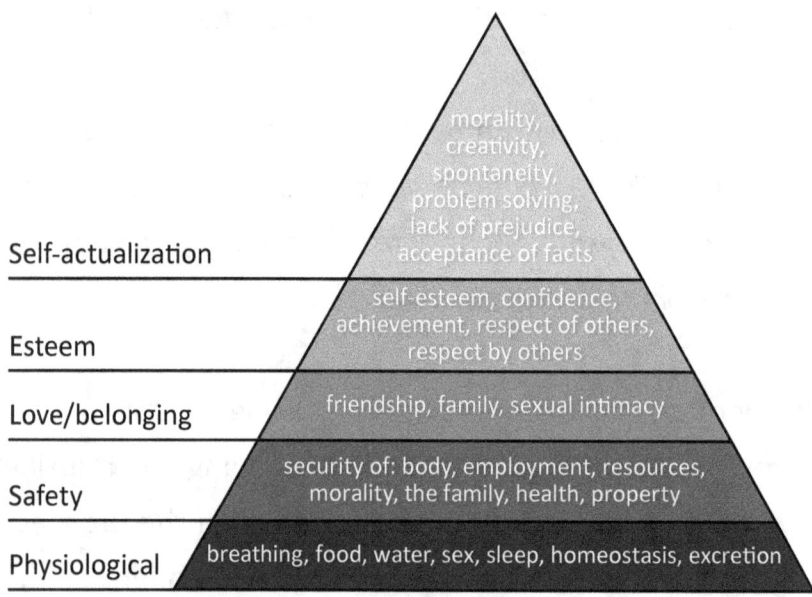

Generally we start at the bottom of the pyramid, and as those needs are met we move up to each successive higher level. However, at every level we are pursuing our self-interest. We get a payoff from achieving anything in the pyramid even if some things look like they are selfless.

It is a fatal flaw if an economic theory makes the assumption that people will act in a particular way simply because they are expected to do so. (How did you overlook this, Mr. Marx? Well, you have quite a bit of present-day company.) An economic structure and the laws and regulations that implement it are only viable if people believe they offer the opportunity to attain what people want to achieve.

It is opportunity that fosters the incentive to be productive. *Either getting something for nothing or having the fruits of success confiscated destroys the incentive to be productive.* Without productivity there is obviously nothing to consume. A Chinese proverb makes this point: "It is a hungry man who waits for a roasted turkey to fly into his mouth."

Nature has unpleasant ways of eliminating those who follow wishful thinking that is in conflict with the physical or economic laws of nature. There is a certain Mother whom survivors know not to mess with.

9 Ideal Idealism

Idealists want a better life for everyone. Few of us would argue with this idea. Unfortunately, many idealists promote policies that are unrealistic or are inconsistent with human behavior. In so doing they ultimately achieve results that are the opposite of what they seek. These policies are generally based on the idea that to help the less fortunate, more successful people should contribute ever more of what they have.

This is zero-sum-game thinking in which someone has to lose for someone else to win. It is an easy but inherently wrong answer to a fundamental question: How can people in need be helped in a way that everyone wins?

Falling back on ever-increasing income redistribution diminishes incentive. Government becomes more intrusive, and people take less and less responsibility for their own well-being. Think of a nationalized health care system in which people who take responsibility for maintaining good health end up subsidizing people who don't, where government decides what care people can have and when they can receive it.

Pseudo-idealism is a practice of far-left movements and in particular the radicalism promoted by Saul Alinsky in his book *Rules for Radicals*. Alinsky advised community organizers to falsely claim to profess appealing, idealistic ideas as a tactic in recruiting followers. In so doing the movement takes in many liberals, Progressives, political leaders, unions, educators, and others. This ties in with Alinsky's tactic of wearing sheep's clothing and claiming to support existing government institutions while actually working to eliminate them.[1]

The false idealists pander to low-income and middle-income groups using class-warfare rhetoric on the supposition that everyone has a right to economic equality. They appeal to these groups by advocating that the government take more from the well-to-do and give ever-increasing benefits to those with less. However, for the radical's inner circle, helping lower income people is often a pretense. Often their true objective is to simply gain power.

Realistic idealism is the approach that works. It is not idle speculation. Realistic idealists know that a reasonable investment in education, health care, and other forms of assistance creates an environment of opportunity in which everyone who applies themselves can achieve a measure of success. It does this without violating the rights of people through excessive income redistribution. It allows for failure that generates increased motivation to take responsibility and work toward success. It builds people's self-esteem resulting from their accomplishments. It lessens government intrusion into our lives, reduces government expense, and gives us more freedom to pursue happiness. This is the real deal, and it is a good deal for everyone.

10 Politicians Are Humans Too

We delude ourselves if we don't believe our elected representatives are just like us, namely, that they are motivated by self-interest. Some have enlightened self-interest and find gratification in working toward the long-term betterment of their country. The one thing they all have in common is that they universally claim that this is their intent. However, it is blatantly obvious that, for many, their heart dwells in a different place—they like the job, and they want to keep it. The money is good, and the prestige and power are great. They are often self-delusional, believing they know what is best for other people, and take pride in fighting for it.

The name of the game for these individuals is getting reelected, and to stay in office they seek to buy votes by getting as much as they can for their constituents. They see this as their duty, conveniently overlooking the fact that they are often using other people's money and impairing the long-term best interests of their country.

Takers are a large part of their constituency. As a group these people are less educated and often less motivated.

In addition, this includes minority groups that have been discriminated against in the past. They have a bias toward considering themselves victims and, as such, claim a bigger slice of the pie. What these people generally don't understand is that bingeing on government largesse at the expense of others ultimately comes with a very big hangover. In the end everyone loses.

It is the Producers who strive for wealth that create a wealthy nation. They put forth the effort, investment, take the risks, and invent things. They create new, better, and less-expensive products and services. They create and grow businesses that offer jobs and opportunities for advancement. They generate the wealth that funds government and enables it to provide programs and services, many of which are disproportionately beneficial to the Takers.

If the Takers and their political enablers unwittingly seek to get too much too soon by either over-taxing the providers or serious national overspending, then they cripple the wealth-creation process.

Some deride this logic as "trickle-down economics" and say it doesn't work because there is growing disparity between rich and poor. However, the real test is whether lower-income people are better off than before.

The demagoguery that generates envy and class warfare is damaging to everyone, especially to low-income people who are made to feel like victims. A victim is more likely to feel sorry for themselves at the expense of taking responsibility for making a better life.

This is further exacerbated by defining a poverty level, a level of income below which a person or family is considered poor. This tends to make a person think, "I'm poor because the government says so, and consequently I deserve to get something extra from the government. I'm certainly going to vote for representatives who will work to make this happen."

It is ironic that many who come to this country are happy with their circumstances even though they are below the poverty level. Here "poor" people have cars, TVs, and other things that they could only dream about where they came from. These people don't feel sorry for themselves but see opportunity to have a better life if they are willing to work for it.

What happens when a country reaches a point where the Takers, unrealistic idealists, and subversives become the voting majority? It is certainly a fork in the road with huge consequences. Hopefully enough people will understand what is truly in their best interest and sense will prevail over feel-good emotional decisions. Hopefully the damage done by the current administration will be enough of a poke in the pants to get enough people motivated to get our nation back on a sound path to prosperity. As things are now, we are dancing along the brink.

Our only hope is that the electorate will be smart enough to put the right kind of leaders into office. It is up to us.

11 Honesty About Dishonesty

Is honesty important? In a democracy it is essential because we the people elect our leaders. To make good choices, we need truthful information. There are two parts to this: leaders and others who provide information must care about and tell the truth, and the electorate must care about hearing the truth.

In the United States, many people assume that what officials tell us is true, except possibly in political campaigns, when the truth may be shaded a bit now and then. However, under our right to free speech, lying is permitted unless it leads to harm. This is as it should be. It would be a nightmare if Big Brother was scrutinizing the correctness of everything we say.

Unfortunately, far too many people don't care about the truth as long as they are getting what they want. Over the last century, Progressives and others on the left have promoted the idea that the betterment of society by any means is justified. As a result this notion has become increasingly accepted. If a poll were taken, it is likely that a large segment of the American population would agree that "the end justifies the means." So it is not surprising that we elect many leaders that believe in this principle.

President Obama is a prime example as he repeatedly demonstrates a loose relationship with the truth. He regularly gives forth misinformation that amounts to either negligent ignorance of the facts or outright lying to the American people. He is arguably the most deceptive president in recent history and probably of all time. The following are some of his deviations from the truth as listed by *Human Events*[2] and others.

Americans want higher taxes: During the debate over raising the debt ceiling, President Obama said that 80 percent of Americans support including higher taxes as part of the deal. But a Rasmussen poll taken the same week showed that only 34 percent believe a tax hike should be included in a debt-ceiling agreement.

Mother denied health insurance: During his presidential campaign, Obama said that his mother died of cancer after being denied coverage for a preexisting condition. He used her image in a campaign ad, repeated the claim in debates, and used the same rhetoric as president when he tried to sell ObamaCare to the American people. But a new book by *New York Times* reporter Janny Scott says that Obama's mother, Ann Dunham, had health insurance through her employer and was only denied disability insurance.

Tax restraint for middle and lower class: Obama pledged during his campaign and throughout his presidency not to raise taxes on families making less than $250,000. However, ObamaCare has $800 billion in new taxes, much of which will hit this group. In addition, 75 percent of the individual mandate tax will land on those making less than $250,000, which includes young adults and middle-income families.

Cost of ObamaCare: Obama promised that ObamaCare would not cost more than $900 billion over ten years. After the health care bill was passed, the General Accounting Office determined that it would actually cost twice as much. In addition, since states are no longer required to cover the cost of additional Medicaid recipients, the federal government will have to pay out an additional $500 billion. It is now estimated that the total cost will exceed $2.6 trillion.

Shovel-ready jobs: When Obama was selling his $787 billion stimulus package, he consistently bragged about how shovel-ready construction jobs would be funded across the nation. Even the president later admitted that was a lie, when he told the *New York Times*, "There's no such thing as shovel-ready projects."

Keep your doctor: President Obama repeatedly pledged that under his health care measure, Americans would be able to keep their doctors. However, with rising costs, many employers will dump their health care plans and force workers into the state insurance exchanges (unless you belong to one of the unions getting ObamaCare waivers). A <u>survey by McKinsey & Company</u>[3] found that more than 30 percent of companies will discontinue coverage for their workers. In addition, as ObamaCare causes insurance companies to go out of business, policy holders will be forced to buy other insurance. In any case many people will have to pay more for their medical insurance because the government will require policies to cover more conditions, some of which may not even apply to the policy holder, like a single male having to carry maternity coverage.

No lobbyists: During the 2008 presidential campaign, Obama said: "We have the chance to tell all those corporate lobbyists that the days of them setting the agenda in Washington are over... I don't take a dime of their money, and when I am president, they won't find a job in my White House." At least a dozen former lobbyists got top jobs in his administration at the beginning of his presidency, according to *Politico.* National Public Radio reported that the Obama administration was granting waivers to lobby-ists to circumvent the ban.

Foreign money in campaigns: During his 2010 State of the Union address and again during the 2010 midterm elections, Obama railed against foreign money influenc-ing US elections. The only problem was that there was no evidence to support the charge. Associate Justice Samuel Alito, who was in the audience, silently mouthed, "Not true."

Arizona immigration law: During the battle over Ari-zona's immigration law, President Obama said: "Now sud-denly if you don't have your papers and you took your kid out to get ice cream, you can be harassed, that's some-thing that could potentially happen." Uh, actually, Mr. President, it couldn't. The law would allow law enforce-ment officials to inquire about immigration status only when there is suspicion of a crime being committed.

Transparency: Obama pledged that transparency would be a top priority, but his administration refused to grant one-third of the Freedom of Information Act requests, according to an Associated Press analysis. He also was dishonest about transparency when he said that health-care negotiations would be televised on C-Span and that he would wait five days to sign a bill so people would have a chance to read it online. As we know, quite the opposite occurred.

Increased oil production: The administration seeks to take credit for the fact that United States oil and gas production has increased during its tenure. The truth is, the administration has thwarted oil and gas development on federal lands where production has declined, according to the Institute for Energy Research[4] (IER). However, this has been more than offset by increased oil and gas production on private and state lands. Furthermore, much of the increased production today is the result of actions taken in the Bush administration, since it takes about ten years to bring a new oil tract into production.

Obama and his supporters believe that it is important to rapidly promote the development and use of green sources of energy, and to discourage the use of fossil fuels. While green energy is a desirable goal, it is unlikely that most people want to incur the expense of forced energy development at a high cost to the United States economy and their pocketbooks. So to avoid taking heat for this, Obama falsely takes credit for expanding US fossil-fuel production.

Energy reserves: Obama stresses the importance of developing green energy now by stating that the United States has oil reserves of only 2 percent of the world supply. But the IER reports[5] that the United States has its own recoverable oil reserves that will last it for many decades, not to mention that the United States has more fossil-fuel reserves than any other country.

Government regulation: Obama said on January 25, 2011, in the State of the Union address: "When we find rules that put an unnecessary burden on businesses, we will fix them." Yet over the course of the year that ensued, a Heritage Foundation study[6] found that the Obama administration enacted thirty-two new "major" regulations—rules that individually carry an estimated price tag of $100 million or more. These measures stand to cost the US economy $10 billion a year, along with an additional $6.6 billion in first-time implementation costs.

Federal spending: In a speech in Des Moines, Iowa, Obama said, "Federal spending since I took office has risen at the slowest pace of any president in almost sixty years." This is based on a manipulation of the facts that results in an annual spending growth rate from 2010 to 2013 of 0.4 percent. However, the actual rate of spending growth has actually been about 3.0 percent. During Obama's three years in office, the national debt has gone up by five trillion dollars, which is more than the four trillion increase during President Bush's eight years. From 1994 to 2008 federal spending was 18 percent to 21 percent of the economy.

But under Obama spending has increased to 24.1 percent. Also under Obama the federal debt has gone from 40.5 percent of the economy to 74.2 percent of the economy.

Taxes on the Middle Class: Obama claims that under Mitt Romney's proposed tax plan, middle and lower class earners will pay as much as $2,000 a year more in taxes to give the wealthy a large tax break. This is based on a single study by the Tax Policy Center, a liberal think tank. According to a Wall Street Journal article:[7]

> ... The Tax Policy Center admits that "we do not score Governor Romney's plan directly as certain components of his plan are not specified in sufficient detail." But no matter, the study plows ahead to analyze features of the Romney plan that aren't even in it.

The article goes on to explain in great detail why the study is bogus. Of course, this does not keep Obama from using the study to make statements that are egregiously false.

Elitist leaders use lies and deception believing they can make better decisions for us than we can for ourselves. This is arrogance gone wild and kicks dirt in the face of democracy. It's a long way from George Washington, who admitted chopping down a cherry tree saying, "I cannot tell a lie." The truth is, when it comes to honesty, we've been headed in the wrong direction.

Most Americans are reluctant to call their president a liar, although by any definition of the word he is. This is not a partisan statement. It is simply the truth. The dictionary defines a lie as:

- *To say something that is not true in a conscious effort to deceive somebody;*
- *To give a false impression;*
- *A false statement made deliberately;*
- *A false impression made deliberately.*

The president has vast resources for getting his facts straight. So when he tells us things that are clearly untrue or are calculated to seriously mislead, he is deliberately lying to us. All Americans, regardless of party or political persuasion, should be appalled that the holder of our highest office is so dishonest and manipulative.

If we tolerate deception by our leaders, we deserve to get what we get in deceit of the pants.

12 Change for the Better

Even if we elect a more insightful administration and representatives, what can be done to fix those things that are
dysfunctional? Change in itself is not the answer because
change might make things worse instead of better.

For example, the Obama health care legislation was
enacted with blatant disregard for normal legislative procedure. The messy operation was passed off as normal
legislative "sausage making." Not surprisingly we ended
up with a national health care plan that promises to be
a catastrophe. This was not "Change we can believe in."
Instead we got change that is unbelievably bad. The new
system does not address the real drivers of health care
costs. It will ultimately reduce the quality of health care
and incur enormous new costs. It was justified by rigged
accounting that would have put people in private business in jail—not to mention its impact on our freedom to
choose. It introduces unprecedented government coercion by requiring everyone to buy health insurance.

Further this administration has instigated a massive
amount of new business-stifling regulation and an enormous

increase in the national debt. Instead of bringing people together as he had promised, Obama has fanned the flames of class warfare.

We should seek change only if it produces beneficial results that substantially outweigh its costs or side effects. With this in mind, I will now look at some major challenges and discuss possible solutions. Many of our nation's problems are interrelated, so fixing one often has beneficial effects on others.

13 Challenge: Massive Federal Debt

The national debt is a ravenous plague that, if not addressed, will grow until it is no longer manageable, and the country will be consumed by it. As of end of <u>2011 the debt</u>[8] was $14,764,000,000, and it is now greater than our total national output. The debt is equal to $47,400 for every man, woman, and child in the United States. In 2011 the interest on the debt was $230 billion. This is **$630 million dollars a day**, all of which has to be borrowed. Currently, the US government keeps interest rates low by printing hundreds of billions of dollars. But this undermines our currency and cannot continue without serious consequences. And when interest rates rise to more normal levels, the United States will be paying over **a billion dollars a day** in interest.

Simple mathematics tells us that in time every dollar of federal revenue will be needed just to pay the interest on the debt. But before that, the debt will grow to such a size that lenders will start to lose confidence in getting their money back. When interest rates begin to rise dramatically, a downward spiral begins. And when it happens, it happens at warp speed.

This is currently happening with Greece and other European countries that have spent excessively. In just eleven months in 2011 the interest rate on Greek ten-year bonds skyrocketed from 12 percent to an astounding 34 percent. Greece is a small country and within the capability of other euro-zone countries to bail out. However, the United States is so large that no one will be able to save us. There will no longer be money to run the federal government, pay for defense, or pay for any other government service. The only money the government will have is money that it prints, and the result will be hyperinflation in which money becomes so worthless that it takes bundles of dollars just to buy a loaf of bread. The result is national collapse. This is no theory. It has happened in other countries in the past.

Another factor to be noted is that historically, when a country's debt exceeds its annual output (Gross National Product), its ability to grow declines dramatically. According to a study called Growth In The Time Of Debt,[9] GNP growth typically decreases by 1 percent or more when national debt exceeds 90 percent of GNP. The United States is now beyond that point, so it is no wonder that we are having so much difficulty extracting ourselves from recession. Recently, there has been optimism that the United States unemployment rate is going down, which would seem to contradict a stagnant growth scenario. However, a recent government report[10] found that millions of the unemployed are not getting jobs but instead are filing for disability as their unemployment benefits run out.

There are only two effective ways to address this problem: reduced government spending and vibrant economic growth. These two objectives must proceed until the tax revenues generated from growth in the economy equals the amount the government spends. This is the point at which our national bleeding stops. The next phase is to start paying down the debt by spending less than the government takes in. Of course, this is a fantasy unless other improvements are made in how we operate as a country.

Some say that another component of addressing the problem is increasing taxes on the rich. However, this is not only an flagrant violation of the rights of this group, but it also doesn't solve the problem. Currently, the top 1 percent of income recipients pays 38 percent of the federal income tax. They also pay the highest tax percentage despite taking advantage of various incentives government has built into the tax code.

According to IRS data for 2007, there were about 391,000 households with income greater than $1 million, and they had aggregate taxable income of about $1 trillion. If the top 1 percent were taxed at 100 percent of their income, the federal government would take in an additional $1 trillion, which would only put a dent in the government's current excessive spending binge. It wouldn't even cover last year's excess spending of $1.3 trillion. Of course, this level of taxation would be insane; the top 1% would disappear as fast as snow on a hot stove, along with their investment capital, spending, jobs, talent, and a big chunk of the economy.

Of course, the richest 1 percent might be taxed a bit more than they are now, but the impact on national debt would be trifling, and risk further depressing the economy. The politics of fostering envy and class warfare is waged for political gain. The people who do so apparently have little understanding of economics or how to foster national prosperity and a better standard of living for all. It is ironic that this group includes some professional economists, academics, and individuals who are supposedly highly educated and teach at prestigious schools.

14 Challenge: Broken Tax System

The federal tax system is an inefficient, costly, unfair mess. An obvious way to improve the government's finances without raising taxes is to implement a vastly improved tax system.

The current system is rife with problems:

- *It is costly to administer and enforce. The IRS budget for 2010 was over $12 billion. But this is a drop in the bucket compared to the cost of compliance for individuals and businesses.*

- *According to a* <u>study by the Laffer Center</u>,[11] *it is estimated that to comply with federal income taxes, taxpayers have compliance expenses of up to thirty cents in addition to every dollar of tax they pay. This amounts to a staggering $431 billion a year to do the necessary accounting and related compliance work. As a result, the United States suffers from billions of man-hours of lost productivity. And this doesn't include the inefficiencies that result from less than optimal business decisions made in an effort to minimize the amount of tax* *that needs to be paid. According to the Government Accounting Office, this cost an additional $265 billion to $663 billion in 2005. At present this is a trillion-dollar hit to the economy.*

- *The code favors certain institutions, industries, and individuals (those that can afford lobbyists and high-priced tax experts) at the expense of everyone else. Those with influence have been the winners while other taxpayers are taxed unjustly.*

- *It encourages gaming the system in order to avoid taxes and creates conflict between people and their government. People who pay their taxes fully end up paying a disproportionately higher amount than those who fudge wherever they can.*

- *People consider the current tax system unfair, and an enormous amount of tax goes unpaid. In 2001 the IRS's taxpayer advocate stated that individuals underpaid their taxes by $345 billion. The result is that those that did pay their taxes ended up paying 32 percent more tax than they would have needed to otherwise. A 2011 study[12] at the University of Wisconsin-Madison concluded that the tax gap is now $450 billion to $500 billion.*

- *Income tax compliance costs are a much greater burden on lower income people.*

Income Distribution of Federal Individual Income Tax Compliance Costs

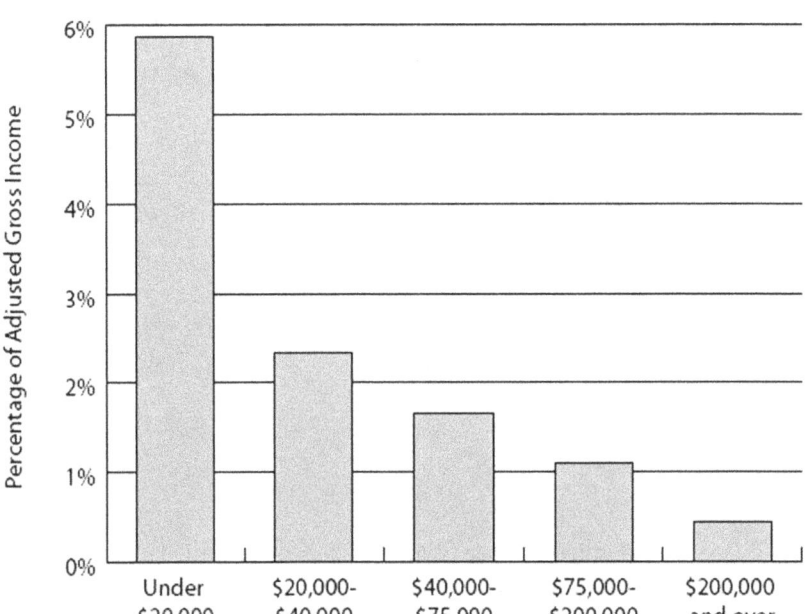

Source: Tax Foundation, Internal Revenue Service

- *It robs citizens of leisure time and peace of mind. Few people would consider an IRS audit a pleasant experience. Unless the taxpayer is represented by an expert (and expensive) tax consultant, the playing field is far from level. Without this help, one is taking a chance, like swimming with sharks.*

- *The US tax code and the added IRS regulations are more than 16,000 pages. If the tax cases and other tax code related documents are added to this, there are 75,000 pages in the Commerce Clearing House tax manuals. The regulations are so vast and complex no one can understand them completely. Here is a sample of one small section of the code that paints the picture. However, you may want to skip over it and keep your sanity.*

Sec. 108. Income from discharge of indebtedness
  (a) Exclusion from gross income
    (1) In general
    Gross income does not include any amount
    which (but for this subsection) would be in-
    cludible in gross income by reason of the
    discharge (in whole or in part) of indebted-
    ness of the taxpayer if -
      (A) the discharge occurs in a title 11
      case,
      (B) the discharge occurs when the taxpayer
      is insolvent,
      (C) the indebtedness discharged is qualified
      farm indebtedness,
      (D) in the case of a taxpayer other than a
      C corporation, the indebtedness discharged
      is qualified real property business indebt-
      edness, or
      (E) the indebtedness discharged is qualified
      principal residence indebtedness which is
      discharged before January 1, 2010.
    (2) Coordination of exclusions
      (A) Title 11 exclusion takes precedence
      Subparagraphs (B), (C), (D), and (E) of
      paragraph (1) shall not apply to a dis-
      charge which occurs in a title 11 case.
      (B) Insolvency exclusion takes precedence
      over qualified farm exclusion and qualified
      real property business exclusion Subpara-
      graphs (C) and (D) of paragraph (1) shall
      not apply to a discharge to the extent the
      taxpayer is insolvent.
      (C) Principal residence exclusion takes
      precedence over insolvency exclusion unless
      elected otherwise.- Paragraph (1)(B) shall
      not apply to a discharge to which paragraph

(1)(E) applies unless the taxpayer elects to apply paragraph (1)(B) in lieu of paragraph (1)(E).

(3) Insolvency exclusion limited to amount of insolvency In the case of a discharge to which paragraph (1)(B) applies, the amount excluded under paragraph (1)(B) shall not exceed the amount by which the taxpayer is insolvent.

(b) Reduction of tax attributes

(1) In general

The amount excluded from gross income under subparagraph (A),

(B), or (C) of subsection (a)(1) shall be applied to reduce the tax attributes of the taxpayer as provided in paragraph (2).

(2) Tax attributes affected; order of reduction Except as provided in paragraph (5), the reduction referred to in paragraph (1) shall be made in the following tax attributes in the following order:

(A) NOL

Any net operating loss for the taxable year of the discharge and any net operating loss carryover to such taxable year.

(B) General business credit

Any carryover to or from the taxable year of a discharge of an amount for purposes for determining the amount allowable as a credit under section 38 (relating to general business credit).

(C) Minimum tax credit

The amount of the minimum tax credit available under section 53(b) as of the beginning of the taxable year immediately following the taxable year of the discharge.

(D) Capital loss carryovers

Any net capital loss for the taxable year of the discharge and any capital loss carryover to such taxable year under section 1212.

(E) Basis reduction

    (i) In general

The basis of the property of the taxpayer.
(ii) Cross reference
For provisions for making the reduction
described in clause
(i), see section 1017.
(F) Passive activity loss and credit carryovers Any passive activity loss or credit
carryover of the taxpayer under section
469(b) from the taxable year of the discharge.
(G) Foreign tax credit carryovers
Any carryover to or from the taxable year
of the discharge for purposes of determining the amount of the credit allowable under section 27.
(3) Amount of reduction
(A) In general
Except as provided in subparagraph (B), the
reductions described in paragraph (2) shall
be one dollar for each dollar excluded by
subsection (a).
(B) Credit carryover reduction
The reductions described in subparagraphs
(B), (C), and (G) shall be 33 1/3 cents for
each dollar excluded by subsection (a). The
reduction described in subparagraph (F) in
any passive activity credit carryover shall
be 33 1/3 cents for each dollar
excluded by subsection (a).
(4) Ordering rules
(A) Reductions made after determination of
tax for year
The reductions described in paragraph (2)
shall be made after the determination of
the tax imposed by this chapter for the
taxable year of the discharge.
(B) Reductions under subparagraph (A) or
(D) of paragraph (2) The reductions described in subparagraph (A) or (D) of paragraph (2) (as the case may be) shall be
made first in the loss for the taxable year
of the discharge and then in the carryovers

to such taxable year in the order of the
taxable years from which each such carryover arose.
(C) Reductions under subparagraphs (B) and
(G) of paragraph (2) The reductions described in subparagraphs (B) and (G) of
paragraph (2) shall be made in the order
in which carryovers are taken into account
under this chapter for the taxable year of
the discharge.
(5) Election to apply reduction first against
depreciable property
(A) In general
The taxpayer may elect to apply any portion
of the reduction referred to in paragraph
(1) to the reduction under section 1017 of
the basis of the depreciable property of
the taxpayer.
(B) Limitation
The amount to which an election under subparagraph (A) applies shall not exceed the
aggregate adjusted bases of the depreciable
property held by the taxpayer as of the beginning of the taxable year following the
taxable year in which the discharge occurs.
(C) Other tax attributes not reduced Paragraph (2) shall not apply to any amount to
which an election under this paragraph applies.
(c) Treatment of discharge of qualified real
property business indebtedness
(1) Basis reduction
(A) In general
The amount excluded from gross income under
subparagraph (D) of subsection (a)(1) shall
be applied to reduce the basis of the depreciable real property of the taxpayer.
(B) Cross reference
For provisions making the reduction described in subparagraph
(A), see section 1017.
(2) Limitations
(A) Indebtedness in excess of value

The amount excluded under subparagraph (D)
of subsection (a)(1) with respect to any
qualified real property business indebtedness shall not exceed the excess (if any)
of - (i) the outstanding principal amount
of such indebtedness (immediately before
the discharge), over
(ii) the fair market value of the real
property described in paragraph (3)(A) (as
of such time), reduced by the outstanding
principal amount of any other qualified real
property business indebtedness secured by
such property (as of such time).
(B) Overall limitation
The amount excluded under subparagraph
(D) of subsection (a)(1) shall not exceed
the aggregate adjusted bases of depreciable real property (determined after any
reductions under subsections (b) and (g))
held by the taxpayer immediately before
the discharge (other than depreciable real
property acquired in contemplation of such
discharge).
(3) Qualified real property business indebtedness
The term ''qualified real property business
indebtedness''
means indebtedness which -
(A) was incurred or assumed by the taxpayer
in connection with real property used in a
trade or business, and is secured by such
real property,
(B) was incurred or assumed before January 1, 1993, or if incurred or assumed on
or after such date, is qualified acquisition
indebtedness and
(C) with respect to which such taxpayer makes
an election to have this paragraph apply.
Such term shall not include qualified farm
indebtedness. Indebtedness under subparagraph (B) shall include indebtedness resulting from the refinancing of indebtedness
under subparagraph

(B) (or this sentence), but only to the extent it does not exceed the amount of the
indebtedness being refinanced.

(4) Qualified acquisition indebtedness

For purposes of paragraph (3)(B), the term
''qualified acquisition indebtedness'' means,
with respect to any real property described in
paragraph (3)(A), indebtedness incurred or assumed to acquire, construct, reconstruct, or
substantially improve such property.

(5) Regulations

The Secretary shall issue such regulations as
are necessary to carry out this subsection,
including regulations preventing the abuse of
this subsection through cross-collateraliza-
tion or other means.

(d) Meaning of terms; special rules relating to
certain provisions

(1) Indebtedness of taxpayer

For purposes of this section, the term ''indebtedness of the taxpayer'' means any indebtedness -

   (A) for which the taxpayer is liable, or

   (B) subject to which the taxpayer holds
   property.

(2) Title 11 case

For purposes of this section, the term ''title
11 case'' means a case under title 11 of the
United States Code (relating to bankruptcy),
but only if the taxpayer is under the jurisdiction of the court in such case and the
discharge of indebtedness is granted by the
court or is pursuant to a plan approved by the
court.

(3) Insolvent

For purposes of this section, the term ''insolvent'' means the excess of liabilities over
the fair market value of assets. With respect
to any discharge, whether or not the taxpayer
is insolvent and the amount by which the taxpayer is insolvent, shall be determined on the
basis of the taxpayer's assets and liabilities
immediately before the discharge.

(4) Repealed. Pub. L. 99-514, title VIII, Sec. 822(b)(3)(A), Oct. 22, 1986, 100 Stat. 2373)
(5) Depreciable property
The term ''depreciable property'' has the same meaning as when used in section 1017.
(6) Certain provisions to be applied at partner level
In the case of a partnership, subsections (a), (b), (c), and (g) shall be applied at the partner level.
(7) Special rules for S corporation
   (A) Certain provisions to be applied at corporate level In the case of an S corporation, subsections (a), (b), (c), and (g) shall be applied at the corporate level, including by not taking into account under section 1366(a) any amount excluded under subsection (a) of this section.
      [<<NOTE: Applicability.>> In general.-Except as provided in paragraph (2), the amendment made to this section by P.L. 107-147 shall apply to discharges of indebtedness after October 11, 2001, in taxable years ending after such date. Exception.-The amendment made to this section shall not apply to any discharge of indebtedness before March 1, 2002, pursuant to a plan of reorganization filed with a bankruptcy court on or before October 11, 2001.]
   (B) Reduction in carryover of disallowed losses and deductions In the case of an S corporation, for purposes of subparagraph (A) of subsection (b)(2), any loss or deduction which is disallowed for the taxable year of the discharge under section 1366(d)(1) shall be treated as a net operating loss for such taxable year. The preceding sentence shall not apply to any discharge to the extent that subsection (a)(1)(D) applies to such discharge.
   (C) Coordination with basis adjustments under section 1367(b)(2)

For purposes of subsection (e)(6), a shareholder's adjusted basis in indebtedness of
an S corporation shall be determined
without regard to any adjustments made under section 1367(b)(2).

(8) Reductions of tax attributes in title 11
cases of individuals to be made by estate
In any case under chapter 7 or 11 of title
11 of the United States Code to which section 1398 applies, for purposes of paragraphs (1) and (5) of subsection (b) the
estate (and not the individual) shall be
treated as the taxpayer. The preceding sentence shall not apply for purposes of ap-
plying section 1017 to property transferred
by the estate to the individual.

(9) Time for making election, etc.
(A) Time
An election under paragraph (5) of subsection (b) or under paragraph (3)(C) of subsection (c) shall be made on the taxpayer's
return for the taxable year in which the
discharge occurs or at such other time as
may be permitted in regulations prescribed
by the Secretary.
(B) Revocation only with consent
An election referred to in subparagraph
(A), once made, may be revoked only with
the consent of the Secretary.
(C) Manner
An election referred to in subparagraph (A)
shall be made in such manner as the Secretary may by regulations prescribe.

(10) Cross reference
For provision that no reduction is to be made
in the basis of exempt property of an individual debtor, see section 1017(c)(1).

(e) General rules for discharge of indebtedness
(including discharges not in title 11 cases or
insolvency)
For purposes of this title -
(1) No other insolvency exception
Except as otherwise provided in this section,

there shall be no insolvency exception from
the general rule that gross income includes
income from the discharge of indebtedness.
(2) Income not realized to extent of lost deductions No income shall be realized from the
discharge of indebtedness to the extent that
payment of the liability would have given rise
to a deduction.
(3) Adjustments for unamortized premium and
discount
The amount taken into account with respect to
any discharge shall be properly adjusted for
unamortized premium and unamortized discount
with respect to the indebtedness discharged.
(4) Acquisition of indebtedness by person related to debtor
    (A) Treated as acquisition by debtor
    For purposes of determining income of the
    debtor from discharge of indebtedness, to
    the extent provided in regulations pre-
    scribed by the Secretary, the acquisition
    of outstanding indebtedness by a person
    bearing a relationship to the debtor speci-
    fied in section 267(b) or 707(b)(1) from a
    person who does not bear such a relation-
    ship to the debtor shall be treated as the
    acquisition of such indebtedness by the
    debtor. Such regulations shall provide for
    such adjustments in the treatment of any
    subsequent transactions involving the in-
    debtedness as may be appropriate by reason
    of the application of the preceding sen-
    tence.
    (B) Members of family
    For purposes of this paragraph, sections
    267(b) and 707(b)(1) shall be applied as
    if section 267(c)(4) provided that the fam-
    ily of an individual consists of the indi-
    vidual's spouse, the individual's children,
    grandchildren, and parents and any spouse of
    the individual's children or grandchildren.
    (C) Entities under common control treated
    as related

For purposes of this paragraph, two entities which are treated as a single employer under subsection (b) or (c) of section 414 shall be treated as bearing a relationship to each other which is described in section 267(b).

(5) Purchase-money debt reduction for solvent debtor treated as price reduction

If -

(A) the debt of a purchaser of property to the seller of such property which arose out of the purchase of such property is reduced,

(B) such reduction does not occur -

(i) in a title 11 case, or

(ii) when the purchaser is insolvent and

(C) but for this paragraph, such reduction would be treated as income to the purchaser from the discharge of indebtedness, then such reduction shall be treated as a purchase price adjustment.

(6) Indebtedness contributed to capital

Except as provided in regulations, for purposes of determining income of the debtor from discharge of indebtedness, if a debtor corporation acquires its indebtedness from a shareholder as a contribution to capital -

(A) section 118 shall not apply, but

(B) such corporation shall be treated as having satisfied the indebtedness with an amount of money equal to the shareholder's adjusted basis in the indebtedness.

(7) Recapture of gain on subsequent sale of stock

(A) In general

If a creditor acquires stock of a debtor corporation in satisfaction of such corporation's indebtedness, for purposes of section 1245 -

(i) such stock (and any other property the basis of which is determined in whole or in part by reference to the adjusted basis of such stock) shall be treated as section 1245 property,

(ii) the aggregate amount allowed to
the creditor - (I) as deductions under
subsection (a) or (b) of section 166
(by reason of the worthlessness or par-
tial worthlessness of the indebtedness),
or (II) as an ordinary loss on the exchange, shall be treated as an amount
allowed as a deduction for depreciation
and
(iii) an exchange of such stock quali-
fying under section 354(a), 355(a), or
356(a) shall be treated as an exchange
to which section 1245(b)(3) applies.
The amount determined under clause (ii)
shall be reduced by the amount (if any)
included in the creditor's gross income
on the exchange.
(B) Special rule for cash basis taxpayers
In the case of any creditor who computes
his taxable income under the cash receipts
and disbursements method, proper adjustment
shall be made in the amount taken into account under clause (ii) of subparagraph (A)
for any amount which was not included in
the creditor's gross income but which would
have been included in such gross income
if such indebtedness had been satisfied in
full.
(C) Stock of parent corporation
For purposes of this paragraph, stock of a
corporation in control (within the meaning
of section 368(c)) of the debtor corporation shall be treated as stock of the debt-
or corporation.
(D) Treatment of successor corporation
For purposes of this paragraph, the term
''debtor corporation'' includes a successor
corporation.
(E) Partnership rule
Under regulations prescribed by the Secretary, rules similar to the rules of the
foregoing subparagraphs of this paragraph

shall apply with respect to the indebtedness of a partnership.

(8) Indebtedness satisfied by corporate stock or partnership interest.-For purposes of determining income of a debtor from discharge of indebtedness, if-

(A) a debtor corporation transfers stock, or

(B) a debtor partnership transfers a capital or profits interest in such partnership, to a creditor in satisfaction of its recourse or nonrecourse indebtedness, such corporation or partnership shall be treated as having satisfied the indebtedness with an amount of money equal to the fair market value of the stock or interest. In the case of any partnership, any discharge of indebtedness income recognized under this paragraph shall be included in the distributive shares of taxpayers which were the partners in the partnership immediately before such discharge.

(9) Discharge of indebtedness income not taken into account in determining whether entity meets REIT qualifications Any amount included in gross income by reason of the discharge of indebtedness shall not be taken into account for purposes of paragraphs (2) and (3) of section 856(c).

(10) Indebtedness satisfied by issuance of debt instrument

(A) In general

For purposes of determining income of a debtor from discharge of indebtedness, if a debtor issues a debt instrument in satisfaction of indebtedness, such debtor shall be treated as having satisfied the indebtedness with an amount of money equal to the issue price of such debt instrument.

(B) Issue price

For purposes of subparagraph (A), the issue price of any debt instrument shall be de-

termined under sections 1273 and 1274.
For purposes of the preceding sentence,
section 1273(b)(4) shall be applied by reducing the stated redemption price of any
instrument by the portion of such stated
redemption price which is treated as interest for purposes of this chapter. (f) Student loans

(1) In general
In the case of an individual, gross income does
not include any amount which (but for this subsection) would be includible in gross income by
reason of the discharge (in whole or in part) of
any student loan if such discharge was pursuant to a provision of such loan under which all
or part of the indebtedness of the individual
would be discharged if the individual worked for
a certain period of time in certain professions
for any of a broad class of employers.

(2) Student loan
For purposes of this subsection, the term
''student loan''means any loan to an individual
to assist the individual in attending an educational organization described in section 170(b)
(1)(A)(ii) made by -

(A) the United States, or an instrumental-
ity or agency thereof,

(B) a State, territory, or possession of
the United States, or the District of Co-
lumbia, or any political subdivision thereof,

(C) a public benefit corporation -
    (i) which is exempt from taxation under
    section 501(c)(3),
    (ii) which has assumed control over a
    State, county, or municipal hospital and
    (iii) whose employees have been deemed
    to be public employees under State law,
    or

(D) any educational organization described
in section 170(b)(1)(A)(ii) if such loan is
made -

(i) pursuant to an agreement with any entity described in subparagraph (A), (B), or (C) under which the funds from which the loan was made were provided to such educational organization, or (ii) pursuant to a program of such educational organization which is designed to encourage its students to serve in occupations with unmet needs or in areas with unmet needs and under which the services provided by the students (or former students) are for or under the direction of a governmental unit or an organization described in section 501(c)(3) and exempt from tax under section 501(a).

The term ''student loan'' includes any loan made by an educational organization described in section 170(b)(1)(A)(ii) or by an organization exempt from tax under section 501(a) to refinance a loan to an individual to assist the individual in attending any such educational organization but only if the refinancing loan is pursuant to a program of the refinancing organization which is designed as described in subparagraph

(D)(ii).

(3) Exception for discharges on account of services performed for certain lenders Paragraph (1) shall not apply to the discharge of a loan made by an organization described in paragraph (2)(D) if the discharge is on account of services performed for either such organization.

(4) Payments under national health service corps loan repayment program and certain state loan repayment programs.-In the case of an individual, gross income shall not include any amount received under section 338B(g) of the Public Health Service Act or under a State program described in section 338I of such Act.

(g) Special rules for discharge of qualified farm
indebtedness
  (1) Discharge must be by qualified person
    (A) In general Subparagraph (C) of subsec-
    tion (a)(1) shall apply only if the
    discharge is by a qualified person.
    (B) Qualified person For purposes of sub-
    paragraph (A), the term ''qualified person''
    has the meaning given to such term by sec-
    tion 49(a)(1)(D)(iv); except that such term
    shall include any Federal, State, or lo-
    cal government or agency or instrumentality
    thereof.
  (2) Qualified farm indebtedness
  For purposes of this section, indebtedness of
  a taxpayer shall be treated as qualified farm
  indebtedness if -
    (A) such indebtedness was incurred direct-
    ly in connection with the operation by the
    taxpayer of the trade or business of farm-
    ing and
    (B) 50 percent or more of the aggregate
    gross receipts of the taxpayer for the 3
    taxable years preceding the taxable year
    in which the discharge of such indebted-
    ness occurs is attributable to the trade or
    business of farming.
  (3) Amount excluded cannot exceed sum of tax
  attributes and business and investment assets
    (A) In general
    The amount excluded under subparagraph (C)
    of subsection (a)(1) shall not exceed the
    sum of - (i) the adjusted tax attributes of
    the taxpayer and (ii) the aggregate adjust-
    ed bases of qualified property held by the
    taxpayer as of the beginning of the taxable
    year following the taxable year in which
    the discharge occurs.
    (B) Adjusted tax attributes
    For purposes of subparagraph (A), the term
    ''adjusted tax attributes'' means the sum
    of the tax attributes described in subpara-
    graphs (A), (B), (C), (D), (F), and (G) of

subsection (b)(2) determined by taking into account $3 for each $1 of the attributes described in subparagraphs (B), (C), and (G) of subsection (b)(2) and the attribute described in subparagraph (F) of subsection (b)(2) to the extent attributable to any passive activity credit carryover.

(C) Qualified property
For purposes of this paragraph, the term ''qualified property'' means any property which is used or is held for use in a trade or business or for the production of income.

(D) Coordination with insolvency exclusion
For purposes of this paragraph, the adjusted basis of any qualified property and the amount of the adjusted tax attributes shall be determined after any reduction under subsection (b) by reason of amounts excluded from gross income under subsection (a)(1)(B).

(h) Special Rules Relating to Qualified Principal Residence Indebtedness.-

(1) Basis reduction.-The amount excluded from gross income by reason of subsection (a)(1)(E) shall be applied to reduce (but not below zero) the basis of the principal residence of the taxpayer.

(2) Qualified principal residence indebtedness.- For purposes of this section, the term `qualified principal residence indebtedness' means acquisition indebtedness (within the meaning of section 163(h)(3)(B), applied by substituting `$2,000,000 ($1,000,000' for `$1,000,000 ($500,000' in clause (ii) thereof) with respect to the principal residence of the taxpayer.

(3) Exception for certain discharges not related to taxpayer's financial condition.-Subsection (a)(1)(E) shall not apply to the discharge of a loan if the discharge is on account of services performed for the lender or any other factor not directly related to a decline in the value of the residence or to the financial condition

```
of the taxpayer.
(4) Ordering rule.-If any loan is discharged,
in whole or in part and only a portion of such
loan is qualified principal residence indebted-
ness, subsection (a)(1)(E) shall apply only to
so much of the amount discharged as exceeds the
amount of the loan (as determined immediately
before such discharge) which is not qualified
principal residence indebtedness.
(5) Principal residence.-For purposes of this
subsection, the term `principal residence' has
the same meaning as when used in section 121.
```

What a nightmare. It's understandable if you chose not to read the whole thing—or even the first page for that matter. The above tax code section is just 4,078 words out of the tax code, which, according to a Tax Foundation Special Report,[13] had 9,097,000 words as of 2005. Think of what it would be like to read, let alone comprehend, the whole code, which is 2,200 times longer.

The IRS is not the primary culprit here. Over the years Congress and the executive branch have continually tinkered with the code favoring this group or that, promoting one policy or another, and plugging loopholes here and there. But in addition, taxing income is tremendously complex because there are so many diverse circumstances that affect income, losses, and deductions. That is why trying to tax income becomes a quagmire that is costly and rife with injustice.

Our tax system is such a monstrosity that even the IRS answers questions wrongly 10 percent of the time, according to a report by Freedom Works[14] based on IRS data. Even more galling is that the IRS does not take responsibility if they pass on incorrect information. Yet everyone is held accountable to follow tax regulations to the letter or face penalties. In tax disputes the taxpayer is guilty unless they can prove otherwise. (Whatever happened to our right to the presumption of innocence?)

The IRS regulations are an insane quagmire that is a serious drag on the vitality of US businesses, the economy, and the American people.

There are alternatives:

One possibility would be a constitutional amendment that would discontinue all taxes on income and replace them with a national retail sales tax. The tax rate would be fixed and could only be increased by a two-thirds vote of both houses of Congress and then for only one year.

This would virtually do away with the current tax code, which would be replaced with far simpler procedures for collecting the sales tax from retailers. Other than for these businesses, no one would have to file a tax return.

The elimination of business income tax would bring about a business boom in which companies would vie for employees, resulting in virtually no unemployment. Wages would rise. Without the cost of taxes and tax compliance, the price of products would go down, and reinvestment in companies would increase dramatically. Business decisions would no longer be influenced by tax regulations but instead by what makes the best business sense.

Exports would increase as the basic reductions in costs would make US products more price competitive. The balance of trade would improve as imported goods would cost the consumer more with the sales tax added. This would in turn encourage manufacturing in the United States rather than overseas. Even with the national sales tax, consumers would be better off due to the elimination of tax on income, dividends, capital gains, and estate taxes.

People and institutions would be encouraged to invest as companies could afford to pay higher dividends, and they would no longer be taxed. This would certainly be of significance to pension funds and older people on fixed incomes.

The retail sales tax would also be fairer, as there would no longer be special tax breaks and loopholes for special-interest groups. Government would no longer be picking business winners and losers, nor would lobbyists influence Congress to grant special tax concessions. Congress could stop wasting time in rancorous debate over tax issues.

The federal government could greatly reduce what it spends on tax collection, and the IRS would shrink to a fraction of its current size. The government would no longer be harassing its citizens to collect taxes, at times fining or imprisoning them. Tax evasion would be virtually eliminated, and the government would collect close to 100 percent of what is due.

While this is not the only possibility for an improved tax system, it does a great deal to rectify the deep flaws of the current national income tax system. Maybe just as important as anything, it does not pit one group of citizens against another. And it makes every voter sensitive to the cost of government and how much government we want to have.

The growth in prosperity from this new tax system would enable people throughout the country to have better employment opportunities and more money to spend for products and services. In turn, government revenues on those purchases would swell. This in turn would generate added revenue to pay down debt and lower the government's interest expense. This virtuous cycle would make the United States and its people increasingly prosperous compared to our current situation in which we are headed to stagnation and worse.

However, the process of converting to a completely new tax system would need to be done with care to avoid a number of potential costs like a drop in federal revenue, lost employment of tax workers, and a hit to the economy. Accordingly, it is worthwhile to at least speculate on some of the significant likely impacts.

Impact of Replacing Current Tax System

		Estimated Savings	
	Current Cost	Cost Reduction	Eventual Savings
Compliance	431,000,000,000	80%	344,800,000,000
Unpaid tax	475,000,000,000	0%	-
IRS Cost	12,000,000,000	50%	6,000,000,000
Business Inefficiency	455,000,000,000	90%	409,500,000,000
Total	**1,373,000,000,000**		**760,300,000,000**

This example assumes that switching tax systems is revenue neutral, and that it is phased in over several years. For the sake of making this example simple, it is assumed that full implementation takes four years, and that there are no savings the first year due to transition costs. Some reductions in tax-worker employment would be offset through normal attrition and by absorption into private business as the economy grows. But it is likely that there would need to be some redeployment assistance for these people. It is also assumed that the savings would increase over the next three years at 33 percent a year. So the savings in the second year would be about $250 billion, $500 billion by the third year, and about $750 billion from then on.

The reason unpaid tax shows no reduction is that the people who are underpaying tax would be then paying it instead of those who are now overpaying currently to make up for the deficiency. The tax system would not only be far more efficient, it would also be fairer.

The cost reduction estimates are for illustration and not based on studies. But the point is that an improved tax system would be a tremendous benefit to business, responsible taxpayers, and the economy.

15 Challenge: Excessive Federal Spending

Over the past several years, the federal government has been on a runaway spending spree that is accelerating at blinding speed. The United States is currently spending $1.3 trillion more than it takes in. Supposedly, this is done on the theory that spending will cause businesses to expand and hire more people who, in turn, will generate more taxable income. The problem is that things don't work that way.

It is foolish to expect that most politicians will exercise spending restraint. Spending reductions happen in little bits from time to time, but the histories of our country and others show irrefutably that the incentives to spend are overwhelming. Furthermore, Congress usually fails to investigate whether a need is already being met by an existing program before enacting a new one that addresses the same thing. Legislators like to demonstrate to their constituents that they are doing things for them, so one program gets piled on another.

A central cause of overspending is this extensive duplication and overlap in government programs and agencies. For more than a century, members of Congress have known about the duplication problem, but efforts to address it have consistently failed. In 2011 and 2012 the <u>General Accounting Office (GAO) published reports</u>[15] detailing the numerous areas of overlap along with recommendations to eliminate the waste.

Here are just a few examples compiled by Senator Tom Coburn from last year's report, which lists nearly 430 programs involving duplication across dozens of agencies:

- *100-plus surface transportation programs*
- *88 economic development programs*
- *82 teacher quality programs*
- *56 financial literacy programs*
- *47 job training programs*
- *20 homelessness prevention and assistance programs*
- *18 food for the hungry programs*
- *17 disaster response and preparedness programs*

On February 28, 2012, Senator Tom Coburn submitted <u>written testimony</u>[16] to the Committee on Oversight and Government Reform concerning the most recent 426-page GAO report. His testimony, reproduced in appendix A, gives a straightforward discussion of the report, a history of the duplication problem, and suggests solutions.

The senator has also presented specific suggestions of things that can be done to eliminate waste, duplication, and unneeded programs in *Back In Black: A Deficit Reduction Plan*, highlights of which are given in appendix B. The plan projects that the federal government's debt could be reduced by $9.032 trillion over the next ten years. This begs the question: Why isn't the administration and Congress studying this plan and coming to agreement with the parts that make sense to everyone? Common sense would say that it is stupid (or possibly selfish and irresponsible) to ignore this opportunity and instead seek to spend more, borrow more, increase the debt more, waste more, print more money, and tax the rich more.

It is clear that too many of our leaders and the people who elect them simply cannot help themselves. At a minimum, absolute limits must be placed on spending with a constitutional amendment that limits spending to a fixed percentage of GNP. In times of national emergency, this could be increased temporarily by a two-thirds vote of both houses of Congress.

In any event, spending must be scaled back so that it does not exceed tax receipts and does not require an increase in taxes. Everyone knows that this requires restructuring entitlement programs and eliminating or replacing the vast new health care legislation. (The very name *entitlement program* is highly misleading because under the Constitution no one is entitled to anything. The only thing we should be entitled to is what we contribute to these programs plus interest.)

Unfortunately, there are politicians who know well that this has to be addressed but who seek political advantage by falsely claiming these reforms will throw grandmothers out into the street. This rhetoric is despicable, and people who vote these people into office do a great disservice to their country and ultimately to themselves when the programs cease being viable and fail. It is like a fool who feasts on his store of winter food but runs out before spring and starves. It's just plain stupid.

The federal government is arguably the most wasteful, inefficient, and costly institution in the United States. Agencies are continually created and expand ceaselessly.

It is rare that any federal agency, cabinet position, tsardom, program, or regulatory act is eliminated. There is so much duplication and mixed responsibility that if the executive branch were diagramed, the resulting picture would make a plate of spaghetti look organized by comparison. In times of recession private companies reduce their workforce, eliminate things that are not necessary, and take other actions to reduce expense. Not so the federal government, which continues to grow unchecked like Jack's beanstalk—and we know where that led.

16 Challenge: Bloated Government

It is ironic that the Obama administration is concerned that too many Americans are obese when the government itself is grossly overweight. Many departments have a life of their own. They want to grow, expand their authority, make new regulations, think up new things to do and control. They have no competition so they don't have much incentive to work to deliver more service at less cost. They have limited oversight, and they often promote policies based on personal biases.

Here are some suggestions for improving this situation:

- *Require that departments have clear measurable goals.*
- *Periodically subject departments to a cost-benefit analysis that includes monetary costs and economic benefits, impacts on personal freedom, and opportunities and effects on the country.*
- *Require that agencies be evaluated every ten years based on an analysis of their benefit, including any laws they are charged with enforcing. There would be four possible outcomes based on the analysis: Congress*

would vote to continue the agency, eliminate it, change it, or contract its function to private industry. Under this procedure one-tenth of the agencies would be evaluated each year.

Just by putting this process in place, people within agencies would be stimulated to work toward greater efficiency.

A fundamental weakness of government is that its agencies have no competition. They are monopolies. There is a reason why monopolies are not allowed in private industry—namely monopolies are not driven to deliver ever better products and services at the best possible price. It is therefore logical that government should only do what can only be done by it. Everything else should be done by competitive, private enterprise.

Another related problem is that government executives don't have as much pressure to be tough contract negotiators as those in private industry. Businesses know that if they enter into unfavorable contracts they will go out of business. This is not the case with government. As a result, governments often enter into contracts that increase costs that can only be paid for by increased taxes. As we have seen with the pension plans of public employees, this is not a healthy or sustainable long-term strategy.

The pension costs, work rules, and other advantages given to unionized public employees are now creating serious economic problems in many states.

Another important step to shrink the federal government would be a constitutional amendment to clarify the commerce clause of the Tenth Amendment and limit what the government is allowed to do and demand under that clause. Over the years, the commerce clause has been so broadly interpreted that the rights of states and individuals have been badly usurped by the federal government. Further, huge unfunded mandates are continually being imposed on the states and businesses.

The intrusion of the government has been growing to breathtaking levels over the years. For example, forcing everyone to buy a product or pay a tax under ObamaCare. In another case, according to the Institute for Energy Research,[17] oil refiners are being fined $6.8 million for not using cellulosic ethanol that is not even available yet. Or the closing of websites that provide gambling over the Internet. The stupidity of this last item is that it stops nothing, since people who want to gamble can still do so on Internet gambling sites in other countries.

One would think that the nation would have learned from Prohibition that it is insane to ban or otherwise control an action that is basically unenforceable. If there is something that people want and feel justified in doing, they will do it. Prohibitions ultimately become a source of crime by making it highly profitable for criminals to supply the thing that is banned. The costs of attempted enforcement, incarceration, lost productivity, and lost freedom become a millstone around the neck of society.

17 Challenge:
Excessive Federal Regulation

The body of government regulations is truly stunning, according to a 2011 study, "An Annual Snapshot of the Federal Regulatory State."[18] The *Federal Register* that contains current and proposed regulations is 81,400 pages. It covers fifty titles that represent everything involving the government. For example, Title 26, which was discussed above, governs federal income tax. Appendix C gives the complete list of titles, which shows how pervasive the federal government is.

There are almost 4,000 new final rules added to the *Federal Register* every year, about ten new rules a day. Nearly 38,700 rules have been issued since 2001. When a law is passed, it is up to agencies to formulate rules to implement the law. In 2010, 217 bills resulted in 3,573 rules. This is a behemoth that is growing without check, and it heaps an ever more onerous burden on American enterprise, the economy, and the lives of the people.

The Small Business Administration conducted a comprehensive study of the economic regulatory costs of federal rules in 2010. It concluded that for 2009, the costs were a staggering $1.75 trillion. The costs include things such as price-and-entry restrictions, price supports, workplace costs, environmental regulatory costs, and paperwork costs. Of this, $56 billion was for federal agency enforcement budgets, and $1.19 trillion was borne by private industry, state and local governments, other institutions, and private citizens. This was in addition to taxes.

And it keeps getting worse at an accelerating rate. A Heritage Foundation report,[19] "Red Tape Rising," found that since January 2009, 106 new "major" regulations have been enacted at an estimated cost of $46 billion, plus almost $11 billion more in implementation costs.

In fact, the cost of federal regulation is greater than the gross national income of either Canada or Mexico.

For years the federal government has been careless about the amount of burden it has placed on business and the states. To promote various programs without raising taxes, Congress simply passes on costs in the form of mandates or regulations for which others have to spend a great deal of money to comply. Given the current state of vast over-regulation, it is deeply disturbing that the current administration believes what is needed is even more regulation. It has created an environment that is increasingly hostile to business except for some of its green pets.

This is brought about by a new health-care system and other regulations that have potentially huge additional costs for businesses. These things do not encourage business expansion. The country is in a prolonged period of high unemployment. It is ironic that certain pro-regulation political leaders complain that businesses are not hiring enough people or are taking jobs overseas. It is amazing that they are so clueless that regulatory compliance costs large employers $7,755 per employee and small employers $10,585 per employee, according to an SBA study[20] summarized below.

Table 1. Distribution of Regulatory Compliance Costs by Firm Size in 2008 *

Type of Regulation	Cost per Employee			
	All Firms	Firms with <20 Employees	Firms with 20-499 Employees	Firms with 500+ Employees
All Federal Regulations	$8,086	$10,585	$7,454	$7,755
Economic	$5,153	$4,120	$4,750	$5,835
Environmental	$1,523	$4,101	$1,294	$883
Tax Compliance	$800	$1,584	$760	$517
Occupational Safety and Health, and Homeland Security	$610	$781	$650	$520

Now if these folks had ever run a business they would understand immediately that these costs would make a business more reluctant to hire more people than they would otherwise. In fact, a recent poll of business leaders who graduated from Harvard University found that they would be two times more likely to build a new plant over-seas than in the United States.

To survive in a recession companies generally have to cut down on costs, and to do this they reduce their work-force. This causes them to take a hard look at areas where they have more people than needed to get the job done. This process not only keeps a company in business dur-ing hard times but also makes it more efficient and more competitive. This is especially important in being able to compete with companies in other countries.

The current administration has further exacerbated the unemployment problem by making labor increasingly expensive by introducing a monstrous health-care system and a plethora of pro-union and pro-labor initiatives and regulations, some of which are certainly tied to paybacks for political support. A couple examples illustrate the point:

- *The government told Boeing Corporation it can't move a plant to South Carolina where employees are not forced into unions, making manufacturing cheaper.*
- *A union "card check" method has been promoted, which would make it easier for unions to coerce employees to join.*

- *Unions have driven up costs of employment through work rules, pension plans, and wages to where they have destroyed the ability of some industries to compete and are driving some states toward bankruptcy.*

Business people are rational. They must be smart to be successful. In view of the above, a business would be stupid to hire more people than absolutely necessary at present. It is a mark of how blind the current administration is that it doesn't understand this. Its ideology keeps it from seeing that it is trying to defy gravity and the unpleasant results that will ensue.

The administration clearly has the view that, given the chance, business will prey on the public and therefore needs to be subject to stringent governmental regulation. Unfortunately, this was reinforced by the mortgage-backed securities debacle. However, the government played a major role in forcing banks to make housing loans that did not meet banks' normal lending requirements and that buyers could not afford. Further, government officials did not own up to their complicity in the problem. It was far more convenient to blame business people who were, in fact, operating within the law. The entire mess started with a pie-in-the-sky idea that everyone should be able to own a home whether they could afford it or not. This is a stellar example of how the senselessness of unrealistic thinking leads to dire consequences, in this case, the longest recession in US history. And still, many in political office continue to promote programs based on the same kind of stupidity.

Financial institutions were further vilified for giving executives large bonuses. At the same time, the blamers ignored the head of Fanny Mae, a quasi-governmental institution, who backed an avalanche of bad loans, and lost billions of taxpayer dollars. The government response was to enact increased regulations on lenders with the exception of two of the worst offenders, Fanny Mae and Freddie Mac. Furthermore, the legislation was drawn up by Representative Barney Frank, who was one of the major proponents of policies that originally caused the problem. Talk about inmates running the asylum.

And so the Dodd-Frank act was put into law to more tightly regulate banks. Surprise! The more stringent regulations made banks less inclined to make home loans adding to a continued long-term decline in the housing market.

This just added to the negative effect on business of Sarbanes-Oxley, the increased costs to health care of HIPPA, EPA regulations, and a host of other government impediments to business. Keep in mind that American companies have competitors in other countries where wages are lower and regulations aren't nearly as pervasive and costly. Sensible regulations that balance costs with benefits are desirable. But excessive regulation by overly zealous regulators who think they know what is best for us needlessly increases the price of the things we buy, infringes on our freedom, and damages the ability of business to grow and compete.

The growth of federal regulation under the Obama administration has been breathtaking.

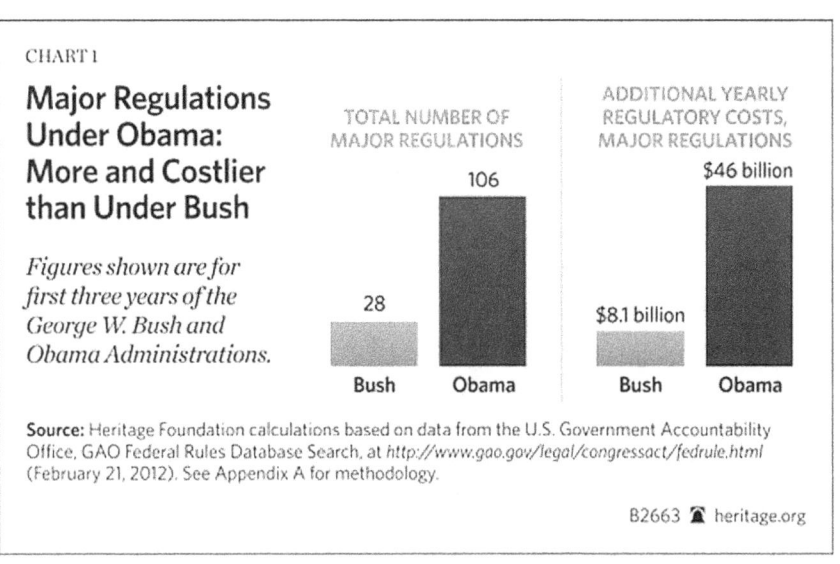

CHART 1

Major Regulations Under Obama: More and Costlier than Under Bush

Figures shown are for first three years of the George W. Bush and Obama Administrations.

TOTAL NUMBER OF MAJOR REGULATIONS

Bush 28
Obama 106

ADDITIONAL YEARLY REGULATORY COSTS, MAJOR REGULATIONS

Bush $8.1 billion
Obama $46 billion

Source: Heritage Foundation calculations based on data from the U.S. Government Accountability Office, GAO Federal Rules Database Search, at http://www.gao.gov/legal/congressact/fedrule.html (February 21, 2012). See Appendix A for methodology.

B2663 heritage.org

Centralized government control of industry is always a disaster, as demonstrated by the dismal performance of the Soviet Union and other such countries. Industries and economies are far too complex to efficiently allocate resources and set prices by any method other than a free-market system. The reason a free market works so well is that production is driven by what each individual actually wants as compared to a top down system in which government functionaries must speculate on what people want. Of course there is the alternative of dictating what people should want, which doesn't work real well either. With this latter approach a lot of warehouses are needed to store all of the stuff no one wants to buy.

18 Challenge: Expensive Health Care

The costs of health care and health insurance have increased dramatically in recent years. There are a number of factors that contribute to this:

- *New medical procedures, equipment, and drugs are expensive to develop and provide.*
- *Enormous court judgments from malpractice lawsuits have made insurance very costly for doctors and hospitals.*
- *The requirement that hospitals provide unpaid-for emergency room care.*
- *Stringent and costly hospital regulations.*
- *Added costs of HIPPA.*
- *Inability to shop for medical insurance across state lines.*
- *Lack of comparison shopping for medical services.*
- *High cost of medical training.*

To make health care more affordable, and coverage more universal, the United States has enacted health-care legislation. Unfortunately, the new system is a nightmare that fails to address the real issues and promises a host of severe consequences.

- *The system doesn't fix any of the problems that are driving up the cost of health care.*

- *It introduces a major increase in socialism in the United States in that the government takes over control of the health-care industry, which represents one-sixth of the country's economy. It calls for a massive redistribution of wealth. It imposes burdensome mandates on businesses and individuals. The legislation was enacted based on invalid assumptions and blatantly phony accounting, such as using ten years of revenue to cover seven years of costs. Massive future costs will result in fiscal disaster—as if current entitlement programs are not major financial problems enough.*

- *A huge new bureaucracy will be needed to administer the system.*

- *The number of doctors will decline as government interferes with their practice of medicine and reduces their compensation.*

- *Medical devices will be taxed, increasing their cost.*

- *Private insurance companies will be driven out of business by taxpayer-subsidized government insurance.*

- *Bureaucrats will have an increasing say as to the health care we can receive over what doctors and patients want.*

- *Bureaucrats have the power to arbitrarily impose mandates that violate constitutional rights, as has happened recently in requiring employers to provide birth control to employees even if they have a religious objection to doing so.*

- *The demand for health services will increase as people who "don't pay the bill" greatly expand the types of care they receive.*

- *It is inevitable that, in time, the quality and timeliness of health care in the United States will decline as it has in every other country where it has been nationalized.*

- *Younger people who need much less health care pay for older people who need much more.*

- *People who are responsible and take good care of their health pay for people who neglect their health.*

- *The system's provision that insurance should cover pre-existing conditions is a "feel good" proposition that is moronic. Insurance is not insurance if the event being insured against has already happened. In reality the system is nationalized medicine disguised as an insurance plan.*

It is hard to imagine a more mangled health-care scheme. It was put together by a small group working in secret and was enacted with bribes and coercion. In addition to special favors given to some states to buy legislators' votes, the record shows that a large number of presidential earmarks were doled out when key votes were taken. Its structure was dictated by ideology and political expedience.

In March 2012, the General Accounting Office issued its *Updated Estimates for the Insurance Coverage Provisions of the Affordable Care Act,*[21] which reports that over the next ten years the insurance **costs of the new health-care plan will be almost double the original estimate of $900 billion**. This means the plan's insurance will cost $1.76 trillion. The total cost of the plan including implementation and other costs is now projected to be $2.6 trillion. And on top of this, there will be significant new costs to states, hospitals, doctors, businesses, and families. At the same time, the GAO says there will be two million fewer people covered by ObamaCare. These people will therefore turn to other types of government assistance. How much more money can America spend and borrow before there is serious national decline?

In essence ObamaCare is a festering wound to the nation that must be excised and replaced with intelligent initiatives that will result in better health care for more Americans at reasonable cost.

The first step is to research all of the factors that make hospital services so expensive. There are some institutions, such as the Mayo Clinic, that have made good progress. There are also hospitals and clinics in other countries that provide quality medical care at far less cost than in the United States. By making a comparison with these institutions we can learn how to make efficiency improvements here.

The second step is to implement changes that will enable hospitals and other care providers to lower their costs and create a competitive environment that will motivate them to do so.

The practice of bloodletting went out long ago. What foolishness to try to cure our health care system by subjecting it to the mega-leach: government folly.

19 Challenge: Energy Insanity

The energy policies of the Obama administration are a farce. They are based on invalid notions about fossil fuels—oil, natural gas, and coal. The policies maintain:

- *The United States has limited fossil fuel resources, and we are in danger of running out of them.*
- *Use of fossil fuels makes the United States dependent on the Middle East and other countries.*
- *Fossil fuels necessarily pollute the atmosphere and lead to global warming.*
- *There is a great urgency to switch to green energy sources—solar, wind, and geothermal.*

Unfortunately, green energy is currently more expensive than fossil fuels. Therefore, proponents believe the federal government must take steps to encourage markets for green energy to develop. The strategy of this administration is to make green energy more attractive by making fossil fuels more expensive and subsidizing solar, wind, and geothermal sources to make them less expensive. Accordingly, the administration has:

- *Suppressed oil-well development on federal land. Among other things, the BP oil-well disaster has been used as an excuse to halt well development in the Gulf of Mexico.*
- *Increased environmental regulations on coal-fired power plants, making their electricity more expensive and the cost of constructing new plants prohibitive.*
- *Blocked oil pipeline development.*
- *Stifled permits for the development of hydrocarbon energy production and resources.*
- *Given billions of dollars to green energy providers and users.*

The president and his green supporters have let their ideology get in the way of facts and have sought to further their cause by attempting to deceive the American people. Now, however, their misguided chickens are coming home to roost, and gasoline prices are starting to rise dramatically, and so is America's ire.

As an example of the president's rhetoric, Obama said: "The United States consumes more than 20 percent of the world's oil, but we only have 2 percent of the world's oil Reserves. Twenty percent we use; we only produce 2 percent. And no matter what we do, it's not going to get much above 3 percent. So we're still going to have this huge shortfall."

This is a blatant distortion of the truth. The facts are very different as reported in a <u>November 30, 2010, Congressional Research Services Report.</u>[22]

It is true that the United States has only about 2 percent of the world's *proven* oil reserves. However this statistic is highly misleading. The United States **has oil, gas, and coal reserves of its own that in all likelihood will last the country for a century or more**. And further, our proven oil reserves would increase substantially if companies were allowed to do more drilling and exploration on federal land.

This is the true picture of the United States fossil fuel status:

Oil Gas and Coal Reserves

- *The United States has proven barrel-of-oil-equivalent (BOE) reserves of oil, gas and coal totaling 972.6 billion BOE, which gives it the greatest fossil fuel reserves of any country in the world.*

- As of 2010, the United States was using 14.3 billion BOE of fossil fuels annually. Accordingly, the United States has proven fossil fuel reserves that are 68 times greater than its current rate of consumption.

- The United States has another estimated technically recoverable oil and gas reserve of 351.5 billion BOE, and this does not include added reserves that will become available as extraction technology continues to improve.

- This is a total of 1,324.1 trillion BOE, which is also greater than any other country in the world.

Oil Reserves

- World oil reserves are 1,354.2 billion BOE, of which the United States consumes 6.85 billion BOE, making the amount we use 0.5 percent of world reserves. The United States more than makes up for that with its production of natural gas and coal. Further, the United States can produce much more of its own oil if the Obama administration would allow it.

Table 6. Reserves of Fossil Fuels Plus Technically Recoverable Undiscovered Oil and Natural Gas

	Total Fossil Fuel Proved Reserves (from Table 5)	Estimated Undiscovered Oil and Gas (Billion BOE, USGS[a])	Total Fossil Fuels[b] (Billion BOE)
Saudi Arabia	309.1	231.3	540.4
Canada	211.4	7.2	218.6
Iran	328.1	114.3	442.4
Iraq	134.8	68.4	203.3
Kuwait	115.3	4.7	119.9
United Arab Emirates	135.8	16.2	152.0
Venezuela	132.4	38.1	170.5
Russia	954.9	293.7	1,248.6
Libya	53.9	10.8	64.7
Nigeria	70.8	63.4	134.2
Kazakhstan	164.1	33.7	197.8
United States	972.6	351.5	1,324.1
China	474.8	28.4	503.2
Qatar	184.8	12.1	196.9
Brazil	42.0	79.4	121.4

a.   U.S. Geological Survey, World Petroleum Assessment, 2000, http://energy.cr.usgs.gov/WEcont/WEMap.pdf; mean values of estimates are used for foreign countries. U.S. number is taken from values in **Table 3**.

To give an idea of the vast potential of United States oil reserves the article "U.S. oil resources: President Obama's non sequitur facts"[23] provides two examples. The exact extent of these reserves will be determined with further exploration, and the economic feasibility of tapping them depends on new and improved means of extraction. However, the technology is advancing rapidly as evidenced by the recent greatly increased natural gas production from shale.

- *The Bakken Formation in North Dakota, South Dakota, Montana, and southern Canada was discovered in the 1980s and 1990s, but because as much as 500 billion barrels of oil was scattered through layers of shale and sandstone it has not been tapped until recently.*

- *There are oil sources that hold tantalizing potential, such as oil shale, that is not yet economically viable but may be in the future. The Rand Corporation says that between 500 billion barrels and 1.1 trillion barrels may exist in the Green River formation in Colorado, Utah, and Wyoming. "The midpoint in our estimate range, 800 billion barrels, is more than triple the proven oil reserves of Saudi Arabia," Rand said in a report.*[24]

This means that even with increasing consumption, the United States is likely to have fossil fuel reserves that will last well over a hundred years without importing a drop of foreign oil. We are hardly in danger of running out of these fuels in the near future. In addition, **the United States now produces more fossil fuel than we consume annually**, so we can be as energy independent as we want to be. This is because oil and gas production on state and private land has more than offset reductions of it on federal lands, as shown in the following Institute for Energy Research[25] graph.

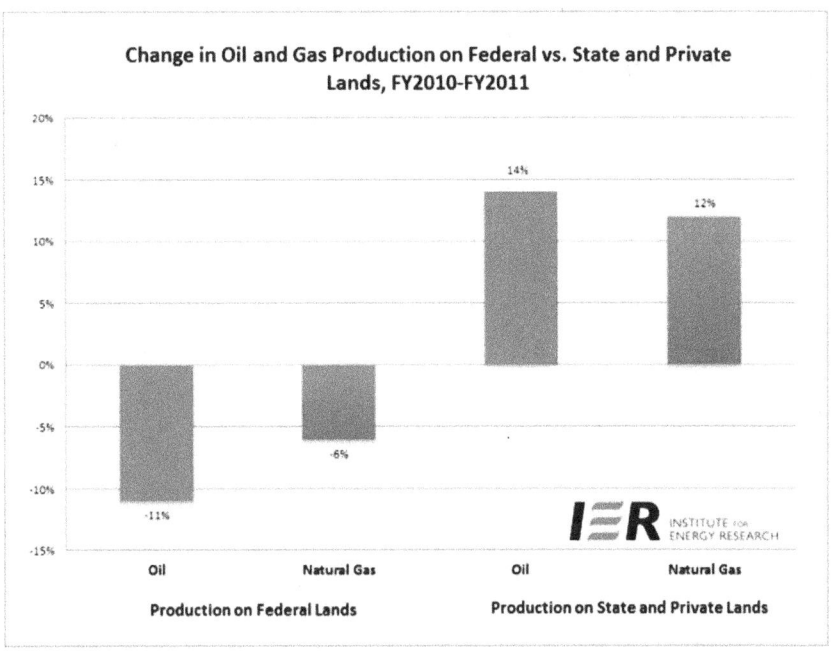

As for the pollution effects of fossil fuels, the technology for reduction of emissions continues to progress and would undoubtedly proceed even faster if some of the money that is being lavished on green energy were redirected to this effort. According to the US Energy Information Administration,[26] federal subsidies in 2010 for wind were $5 billion compared to $654 million for oil and gas. Based on kilowatt hours produced, wind received 85 times more funding than oil and gas.

Fiscal Year 2010 Electricity Production Subsidies and Support (millions)

	Total	Share of Total Subsidies and Support
Coal	1,189	10.0%
Natural Gas and Petroleum Liquids	654	5.5%
Nuclear	2,499	21.0%
Renewables	6,560	55.3%
Biomass	114	1.0%
Geothermal	200	1.7%
Hydropower	215	1.8%
Solar	968	8.2%
Wind	4,986	42.0%
Unallocated Renewables	75	0.6%
Transmission and Distribution	971	8.2%
Total	11,873	100%

Currently the problem with green energy is that it is green—that is, it is not ripe for wide implementation yet. As an example, the cost of solar cells is presently too high compared with electricity from fossil fuels. However, the efficiency of solar cells is continually increasing, and the price has been coming down substantially. Projections are that solar and probably other types of green energy will be in full competitive flower within the next ten to twenty years.

It might be argued that green energy will not develop or the industry will be taken over by countries like China if there is not a concentrated effort to promote it here. This is a spurious argument since experience shows that science and invention move forward even before there is an established market for a product. China heavily subsidizes the solar cell market enabling it to sell much cheaper cells than those produced in the United States. This is fine because the Chinese are spending money the United States and other countries would otherwise have to spend on solar cells now. If and when the time is right, the United States can get into the market. So why spend money unnecessarily now to play on an uneven field?

In 2008, President Obama said, "Under my plan electricity prices will necessarily skyrocket." His plan was to make energy production from fossil fuels far more expensive through taxation and regulation. He has certainly succeeded in making gas more expensive. Doesn't he understand that the increased cost of gas and electricity hits low-income people the hardest? They literally have to give up things in order to cover the extra costs. Doesn't he understand that increased energy costs promote inflation, and depress economic growth?

In the United States, we have enjoyed the benefit of lower fuel prices compared to much of the world. This has given us more freedom to move about, pursue our endeavors, and have a better quality of life. Government manipulations that make things more expensive and add to our debt are deplorable—especially when they are not necessary.

A sane energy approach for the United States is very simple:

- *Promote the continued use and development of fossil fuels.*
- *Support the development of improved emission-reduction methods.*
- *Support the development of green energy technologies but discontinue subsidies. Let the free market determine when it is the right time to switch from one form of energy generation to another.*

After all, we have a hundred years to get there. In much less time than that, the United States will have an abundance of energy from new technology that is advancing dramatically.

- *Solar cell cost has been declining steadily and will be cheaper than hydrocarbon based electricity in less than twenty years. The improvements often come from unexpected directions. For example, Owens-Corning has recently developed thin flexible glass that will make solar cells cheaper and allow them to be installed on curved surfaces.*
- *Room temperature semiconductors will allow electrical devices to operate using only a fraction of the electricity they use today. They will also enable cars, trucks, and trains to travel without contact with the ground, vastly reducing the energy needed. Electrical transmission lines will become far more efficient, saving vast amounts of electricity that is currently lost.*
- *New materials that have superior electrical properties, including graphene, carbon nano-tubes, and selicene, will make the use of electricity far more efficient.*
- *Electricity from atomic fusion will become economically practical.*

20 Challenge: Uninformed, Shortsighted Electorate

If voters had a better understanding of basic economics and the ultimate consequences of their voting decisions, they would put a greater number of wise leaders in office. The leaders that are needed understand the way the world actually works and aren't led by unrealistic and unsustainable ideas of how they would like it to work, which ultimately leads to dire consequences for everyone. The consequences may not hit all of us depending on how long we are around, but watch out, kids!

There is an important subject that is seriously missing from our education system—namely the achievement of personal prosperity, which should cover an understanding of common-sense economics and how it affects individuals. It would also explain how the ongoing health of the economy impacts each individual now and in the future. If more people understand how decisions that favor immediate gratification can hurt them in the long run, then the country will enjoy the benefit of a more insightful electorate. This in turn will result in a preponderance of leaders who have the discipline and wisdom to promulgate policies that will lead to a better life for all. Fortunately, the United States already has many such leaders. But based on the country's current state of affairs, we do not have enough of them in the right places.

Most high schools have standard courses such as physical education and personal health. It would seem that a standard course in personal prosperity is every bit as important.

At the same time, it is important to improve education in the United States. As much as I like the concept of No Child Left Behind, it is a mistake to have the federal government involved in education—not to mention that it does not have a constitutional right to do so. To show how insidious the government's involvement can be, the Department Of Education is proposing national curriculum standards in direct violation of three education laws. If the federal government can control what children are taught, it has an opportunity to promote its own agenda. This kind of influence on the minds of children is a mainstay of Communist and Islamic countries, but it has no place in the United States.

The most important reason to get Uncle Sam out of the classroom is that education will only improve with a free-market, bottom-up approach. Parents, local teachers, and school districts have the most immediate knowledge and interest regarding the education of their kids. School choice is critical so that parents can choose the school for their children, and competition among schools will cause the best to thrive and the worst to close. Of course, these are things that need to be implemented at state and local levels. Another reason federal funds should not be sent to states for education is because the federal government has a bad habit of attaching strings to what it gives out. It would be far better if states got the education money directly from the taxpayer rather than having it collected and doled out by the federal government.

A measure of the voter's opinion of a president is his approval rating. For Obama it has been about 45 percent. What is amazing is that it is that high given his failed economic policies, dishonesty, and unwillingness to take responsibility. He continually blames others for his lack of performance and manipulates the truth to take credit for accomplishments not of his making.

At a time when his country has had record unemployment, massive debt, and an economy that is struggling to recover, Obama spends a historic amount of time going to an unprecedented number of fund-raisers. He has demonstrated that he is so wedded to his ideology that he is incapable of moving to the center to craft effective solutions. He is mired in the idea that "spend, borrow, and tax" is the road to prosperity.

How can almost half of the United States voting public approve of Obama given his record? It is a grave problem when so many voters are so uninformed, indifferent, or guided by shortsighted self-interest. The final result is the type of national implosion currently happening in Greece and potentially in other European countries. However, it should be kept in mind that this is the outcome Alinsky followers are looking for because they believe national collapse sets the stage for their revolution. It is a mechanism by which they promise to take wealth and power from those who have it and redistribute it to the masses. Or what is more likely, take power for themselves, and become a ruling elite.

21 Challenge: Diminishing Personal Freedom

Personal freedom in the United States has been eroding over the last century. This has occurred in a number of areas.

Personal property: The Constitution acknowledges each person's right to have their own property and use it as they wish. If a government takes an owner's property, it must be for a public purpose and the owner must be paid fair compensation. A person's property is everything they own—money, real estate, personal items, and anything else they possess.

This started to change when the Constitution was amended to establish the federal income tax. The government has gone wild increasing tax rates and making them increasingly progressive, taxing business earnings, capital gains, dividends, and estates. Originally the income tax was meant to be used for running the government. But then the welfare state emerged, and money was used for income redistribution programs like welfare, food stamps, and entitlement programs that were made increasingly generous but underfunded. Today upper-income earners are lucky to keep half of what they earn.

The other area of government confiscation is the erosion of the value or utility of real property without compensation. This is done through zoning restrictions that were not in place when the property was acquired or through restrictions based on environmental regulations. The restrictions imposed by the Endangered Species Act have been particularly offensive in this regard. In the Northwest the lumber industry was decimated to protect the spotted owl. To protect fish, water in Oregon's Klamath Basin was cut off to the framers who had been growing crops there for many decades. The people and business that were severely affected received nothing for their loss.

There is an even more concerning trend in which government can seize property without due process. If one's property is associated with a drug-related crime, even if the owner is completely innocent, the property can be taken from them. It is an outrage against justice.

It seems that theft has become perfectly acceptable if the government is doing the stealing.

Pursuit of happiness: The list of things we cannot do gets longer and longer. The government tells us what we are allowed to put into our bodies, purportedly for reasons of public safety. This is true of prescribed drugs and so-called recreational drugs like marijuana. If the government decides a drug is potentially harmful, it is put on a list of controlled substances. If the drug has a government-approved medical use, it can be prescribed by doctors, otherwise its use is completely prohibited. No consideration is given to the enjoyment or other benefits a person might get from the drug or that there is negligible potential harm with its responsible use. It is often assumed substances are bad for us because if we like using them, we will misuse them or we will start using more harmful drugs. Regulators like to overlook it when these assumptions fly in the face of evidence for substances like marijuana.

In any event, taking any substance should not be illegal as long as it does not harm others. Shouldn't each of us decide for ourselves whether the benefits of what we do are worth the costs? Why should we give this power to bureaucrats who are motivated by their own personal biases and who know nothing about us individually? It is preposterous to contend that a small group of government functionaries know what is best for three hundred million unique individuals when it comes to pursuing their happiness.

This is not to say there shouldn't be restrictions on those who are not yet old enough to make informed decisions.

And it might be argued that some people never get to be old enough. However, this is not a reason to restrict responsible people from doing whatever they want to do.

It is telling that in the United States, which prides itself on being "the land of the free," we have a higher percentage of our people in jail than almost any other country, including totalitarian countries like Communist China. This is due in large part to US drug laws.

Freedom from harassment: The United States has instituted numerous regulatory agencies, like the EPA, OSHA, Consumer Protection Agency, FDA, ATF, and others, that see it as their mission to create ever more restrictive regulations in the name of looking out for our safety and the general public welfare. These agencies become fiefdoms that make their own rules and operate with little restraint. They demonstrate little concern for the economic and other impacts they might have on businesses and individuals. These tsardoms have little outside control, and they decide how to impose their will with fines, demands, and imprisonment, which can defy what is reasonable.

Here are two examples:

- *A farmer was cleaning out and restoring a stream that cows had turned into a mire. Someone reported* *his work, and he was visited by environmental authorities. He was told that he was violating a regulation by doing the work and could face penalties. Supposedly he was making the water muddy, and it might affect fish several miles downstream. The authorities did not care that the stream is normally flooded with muddy water whenever it rains or that the farmer was voluntarily working to improve the environment. They forced the farmer to retain an environmental consultant to come up with a remediation plan, which he was then required to implement. The plan and subsequent inspections cost $1,000. Notably the plan was what he was already planning to do.*

- *A couple bought land near a scenic lake and decided to build a home on the property in 2007. However, the EPA ordered a halt, saying the Clean Water Act requires that wetlands not be disturbed without a permit. Further, the EPA said they would impose fines that could be as much as $75,000 a day. There was no reasonable way to challenge the order, and the couple didn't know why the EPA concluded there were wetlands on their lot, which was surrounded by a residential neighborhood with sewer lines and homes. At the risk of incurring millions in fines, the couple went to court. Ultimately the Supreme Court ruled unanimously the couple may chal-*

lenge the EPA head-on in court. Associate Justice Samuel Alito wrote, "Any piece of land that is wet at least part of the year is in danger of being classified by EPA employees as wetlands covered by the act, and according to the federal government, if property owners begin to construct a home on a lot that the agency thinks possesses the requisite wetness, the property owners are at the agency's mercy."

It would take little effort to fill thousands of pages with such stories, some more significant than others. They represent an enormous imposition on American freedom. Authorities generally assume that citizens are inept and have to be lorded over. This leads to abusive authoritarianism and is a major reason why various United States agencies should be reined in or eliminated.

To address these abuses:

- *Each government agency should be subjected to a thorough evaluation of their history of growth in size, cost, and regulations. Then they should either be eliminated or put on a diet.*

- *There should also be an easy-to-use mechanism by which businesses and individuals can register complaints and challenge findings, penalties, and demands.*

22 Challenge: Impediments to Economic Growth

People everywhere are tremendously productive if they believe they will be adequately rewarded for their effort. It is impressive to observe how motivated people often are despite obstacles, many of which are created by governments or exploitive despots.

In the United States the major impediments to economic growth are:

- *Excessive taxation*
- *A decrepit tax system*
- *Excessive regulation*
- *Excessive national debt*
- *Unsustainable federal spending*
- *A so-so educational system*
- *Incentive-dampening policies*
- *Increasing socialism*

One would think that the current federal administration would understand these problems and work to alleviate them. But the opposite is happening. Guided by ignorance, arrogance, and blind ideology our chief executive, his minions, and supporters strive to heap ever more of this burden on the nation's economy, businesses, and people. It is especially disturbing that so many people in the United States appear to be unaware or unconcerned that this is happening and what the implications are.

Many voters are so poorly informed and shortsighted that they vote based on emotion and narrow self-interest rather than on common sense. This is the soft underbelly of democracies that in time leads them into peril. Sometimes a country wakes up and gets itself turned around. These will be the leading nations of the future. But those countries that slide into the abyss of economic failure will fade away or come crashing down as the unrelenting law of natural selection eliminates them. *Stupidity is not a survival trait.*

The United States concerns itself greatly with protecting endangered species. What many don't realize is that this country, its prosperity, its freedoms, and its dream may be the most endangered species of them all.

23 Challenge: Government Gone Rogue

Until the early 1900s, Congress would consider whether it had the constitutional authority to pass a particular law. But early in the twentieth century, Progressives started pushing the idea of social engineering and rule by government experts. The Supreme Court continually blocked schemes that would exceed the federal government's enumerated powers. This led to the infamous effort by President Franklin D. Roosevelt to add six more judges to the Supreme Court in order to pack it in favor of his unconstitutional legislation.

Unfortunately, this intimidated the Supreme Court, which subsequently made rulings in a couple cases that had the effect of vastly liberalizing the interpretation of the Constitution's commerce clause. This has led to the rampant growth of the federal government ever since. The federal government has usurped power to go on a wild spending and regulation spree, the results of which are the serious challenges the United States faces today.

So let us look at what the Constitution says:

- *The federal government has only the powers specifi-cally given to it. The Tenth Amendment to the Constitu-tion states: "The powers not delegated to the United States by the Constitution, nor prohibited by it to the States, are reserved to the States respectively, or to the people."*

- *Some people contend that Section 8 of the Constitution gives Congress the authority to do anything it wants to if it promotes "the general Welfare of the United States." What is actually authorized is the collection of taxes and duties to "provide for the common Defense and general Welfare of the United States." It does not give the Congress the authority to create agencies and pro-grams to promote the general welfare. If this were not the intent of the Constitution and Congress had unlim-ited power to enact anything it wanted, then it would not have enumerated the specific powers of Congress in the rest of Section 8. Furthermore, the Tenth Amend-ment makes this absolutely clear.*

- *People also contend the "necessary and proper" clause in Section 8 gives Congress essentially unlimited author-ity to make any laws it wishes. However, the Constitu-tion actually says that Congress has the authority "to make all Laws which shall be necessary and proper for carrying into Execution the foregoing Powers, and all other Powers vested by this Constitution in the Government of the United States, or in any Department or Officer thereof." It is clear that the authority given to Congress to make laws is limited to those that are proper and necessary for the federal government to exercise its powers that are specifically enumerated in the Constitution.*

The Constitution was designed to prevent runaway federal government. Over the last seventy-five years, Progressives and others on the left have subverted the Constitution and its constraints on the federal government's power. It is no wonder the United States has had the longest recession and slowest recovery in its history given its massive debt, mountainous regulations, enormous bureaucracy, and an administration and Senate that want to pile on more and more spending, taxes, and regulation.

It has been a steady drive toward a financially unsustainable welfare state. It is essentially the same over-promising and over-spending that is in the process of crushing Greece, Spain, Italy, and other countries in Europe. The United States will surely join them in the near future if we continue to be led by our current ideological zealots.

24 Challenge: Imperial Presidency

The Obama administration is arguably the most dictatorial in the nation's history. The President and his people are proceeding in an imperial manner that is inconsistent with expected ethics and their sworn duties.

At his inauguration, the president swore to uphold and defend the Constitution, yet he has taken actions that are contrary to it. Furthermore, he has used lies and chicanery to promote his agenda. For example:

- *To pass ObamaCare, Obama insisted that the "individual mandate" was a penalty and not a tax. In so doing he attempted to greatly increase the scope of the commerce clause of the Constitution. This would have created the presumption of essentially unlimited federal power over personal freedom. The Supreme Court allowed the mandate by calling it a tax. However, for political purposes the administration continues to call the mandate a penalty.*

- *ObamaCare required states to expand Medicaid and to ultimately pay for it or lose all Medicaid funding. This strong-arm attempt to coerce the states was fortunately ruled unconstitutional by the Supreme Court.*

- *ObamaCare requires employers to underwrite the cost of contraception and day-after abortions even though these practices violate constitutional religious freedom of some institutions.*

- *Obama has usurped the right of Congress to confirm appointments by simply claiming he has the right to do so under circumstances in which it has never been allowed before.*

- *Obama has chosen to break his oath of office in which he swore to uphold the laws of the United States by ignoring his duty to enforce immigration laws. Further, he is in violation of the Welfare Reform Act by offering states waivers of the work requirement that is at the heart of that program.*

- *Obama's justice department under Attorney General Eric Holder carried out a program called Fast and Furious that allowed more than two thousand guns to be moved illegally into Mexico. At least one reason for the program was to create a justification for the administration to increase gun control in the United States. Holder has refused for eighteen months to give documents to Congress, which has a constitutional right and duty to investigate the matter. As a result, Holder has been held in contempt of Congress. Obama has attempted to abet Holder by invalidly claiming executive privilege over the documents. Finally, a federal judge, who reports to Holder, is refusing to convene a grand jury to consider the contempt citation. This is blatant conflict of interest and corruption at the highest level.*

- *The Obama administration clearly wants to skew elections using Hispanics who typically vote for Democrat candidates. The evidence:*

  ▶ Refusal to protect the United States border with Mexico despite a continuous flood of illegal immigrants over that border.

  ▶ Suing Arizona for passing laws to improve border protections that are consistent with what the federal government is failing to do.

  ▶ Attempting to stop Florida from ensuring that only legally qualified voters are able to vote.

The president has paid for political support and bought votes for his pet legislation by providing funding to groups and enterprises as payback. Even though the president claims that he opposes earmarks, he has used presidential earmarks far beyond any predecessor in order to buy votes in Congress. A study by the <u>Heritage Foundation</u>[27] found large spikes in presidential earmarks at the times his major bills were voted on as shown in the following graph:

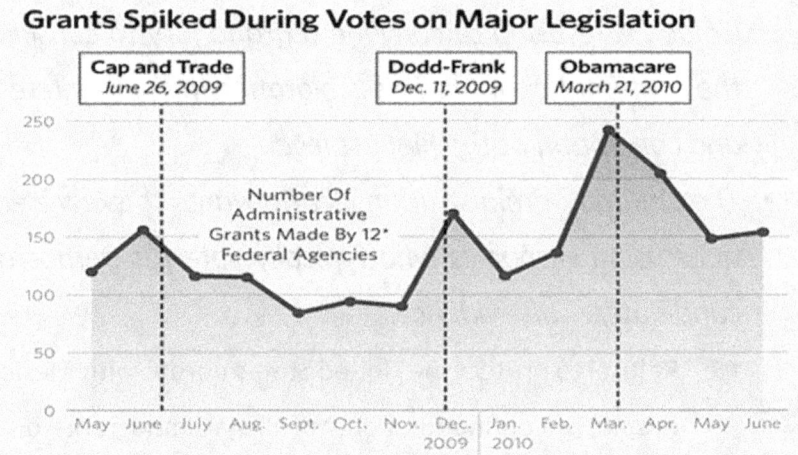

Grants Spiked During Votes on Major Legislation

| Cap and Trade | Dodd-Frank | Obamacare |
| June 26, 2009 | Dec. 11, 2009 | March 21, 2010 |

Number Of Administrative Grants Made By 12* Federal Agencies

* Agriculture, Commerce, Defense, Education, Energy, Environmental Protection Agency, Health and Human Services, Homeland Security, Housing and Urban Development, Interior, Transportation, and Veterans Affairs.

Source: Heritage Foundation research and data from *Grants.gov*.

☎ heritage.org

The president has also been derelict in his duties, spending extensive time playing golf, vacationing, and fund-raising rather than dealing effectively with the worst recessionary period, persistent unemployment, and national debt in the country's history. In his three years in office, the president and the Senate, controlled by his party, have not passed a national budget even though they are required to do so annually by law.

According to the *Washington Examiner*, the president and his family have taken sixteen vacations over his first three years in office. None of these vacations were to the

Camp David presidential retreat, which apparently is not up to their standards. It is astounding that the First Family takes five vacations a year, costing taxpayers millions of dollars, at a time millions of citizens are out of work and America's debts soar.

At great taxpayer expense, Obama has gone to more than 170 fund-raisers, which is far more than all previous presidents combined. He rarely meets with his cabinet and obviously spends little time addressing the many significant challenges mentioned here.

Most recently, the president killed the Keystone XL pipeline project, which would bring oil into the United States, creating thousands of jobs, helping the economy, and making the United States less dependent on foreign oil. Even though all of the required departments had already signed off on the project, he blocked it to garner political support from his green-agenda supporters. There is little question that this is a case of putting his own political ambition above the welfare of the country.

This president and his administration obviously follow the principle that "if they can get away with it, they will do it." Just because a US president has extensive power, it doesn't mean that he has the right to do things for which a private citizen would go to jail. While it is typical for presidents to push the boundaries of their authority, the current administration has taken it to new heights.

It is assumed that a US president would be ethical and have some respect for the Constitution and the separation of powers. However, in Obama we have a president who acts more like a king.

25 The Enemy Within

Our founding fathers had the experience of living under the dictatorial tyranny of King George III of Great Britain. This gave them insight on how to structure the United States so that no one person or group could rise to power and dictate to the country and its people. Accordingly, they crafted a constitution designed to:

- *Establish a federal government with three branches: executive, legislative, and judicial, each with specific limited powers. The branches of government were designed to keep each other in check.*
- *Specify that all powers not specifically granted to the federal government belong to the states and the people of the United States.*
- *Enumerate individual rights that could not be violated by the government.*
- *Provide a procedure for amending the Constitution.*

Under this structure, Congress makes laws within its realm of congressional authority. The president implements those laws and carries out other specific duties. And the Supreme Court and federal courts ensure that the executive branch and Congress were not doing things not permitted by the Constitution.

Accordingly, neither the president nor the courts can make law, regardless of how beneficial they believe it to be. Nor can they change the Constitution. Neither Congress nor the judiciary can administer the law, although Congress has oversight as to how laws are carried out. Neither the president, Congress, nor the courts can violate the rights of states or individuals contrary to the Constitution.

Unfortunately, this structure has been short-circuited by proponents of the welfare state in their effort to address humanistic concerns. The net effect has been to relieve individuals of responsibility for their own well-being and transfer it to the government. This has come at the price of diminished personal freedom and a vast redistribution of wealth.

Along the way, many groups have been hijacked by the radical Saul Alinsky movement, which has made major inroads into unions, education, the Democrat party, and the federal government.

Alinsky, a fan of Lenin, states that any means should be used to achieve this goal as long as the ends required are worth the cost. He states, "The practical revolution-ary will understand Goethe's 'conscience is the virtue of observers and not of the agents of action'; in action one does not always enjoy the luxury of a decision that is con-sistent both with one's individual conscience and the good of mankind."[28]

It might be said that the movement's crowning achievement to date was the 2008 election of Presi-dent Barack Obama and his majorities in the House and Senate. Obama's past associations (e.g. He was tutored by a Communist for nine years[29] and taught radical community organizers[30].) and his actions as President are consistent with Alinsky's goals and methods. A demonstration of this has been the dema-goguery, lies, deceptions, cover ups, and disregard for the Constitution by Obama, his administration, and cohorts in Congress.

Most recently, Obama revised the immigration law saying, "It's the right thing to do," ignoring the fact that he does not have the right to do it under the Constitution. This action is consistent with Alinsky's belief that the only principle to guide government action should be, "For the general welfare." This in effect negates the supremacy of individual rights that is the cornerstone of our nation.

America is on the brink of political and economic crisis. If the radical Leftists are not removed from power, the consequences will be dire indeed. Our hope lies in exposing their true agenda, and repairing the damage that has been done.

26 Challenge: The New Communism

Communism is a utopian idea of a classless, moneyless, and stateless social order in which the means of production are owned in common by the working class, and everything is essentially shared in common. It is arrived at by replacing capitalism with socialism, under which everyone has both social and economic equality. To achieve this goal, property and power are taken from those who have them, and they become the province of the masses, or as history shows, the ruling elite. A significant aspect of Communism is that any action is justified in order to achieve its goals, including the denial of human rights, deception, theft, and murder.

Supposedly a Communist system would produce such abundance that the competition among people for resources and goods would vanish. As we know, the theory has proved to be an abject failure. Communist regimes have slaughtered millions of their people in the name of progress, and have delivered a dismal standard of living for their people. Only China has recently achieved improved standards of living, and that is because it has started to embrace capitalism. However, life for Chinese peasants remains dismal, and the country is rife with corruption.

But the true goal of totalitarian socialism is the acquisition of power as promulgated by Lenin. A leading proponent in the twentieth century was Saul Alinsky, who died in 1972. He made a point of not naming his movement so that it would remain innocuous and unidentifiable. In fact, he counseled his devotees to disguise themselves in order to appeal to whatever community they seek to organize. In this way they are accepted, and can surreptitiously influence the community to rise up at the time for rebellion, or at least not oppose it.

Alinsky's objective was to fundamentally change the United States from a capitalist country to a socialist one by taking power from the Haves, and giving it to the Have-Nots. In his book *Rules for Radicals*, published in 1971, he explains, "how to create mass organizations to seize power, and give it to the people." These organizations are groups of people that are subverted by his radical community organizers.

Alinsky believed that giving power to the people requires a revolution in which using any means is justified as long as it leads to the power to transform America. In essence, this is the new Communism. It is a more refined tactic than used in the past in that it follows a stealth strategy for taking control of the institutions of the United States from within. In the US, Progressives and other groups have been sucked into this movement. Many probably do not fully understand what they are into.

Here are some things to consider:

- *The Democrat Progressive Caucus of the United States Congress has seventy-six members, the largest caucus in the Democrat party. It is not hard to spot Alinsky Progressives because they regularly distort the truth to disparage their opposition or to deceive the general public—a standard Alinsky tactic.*

- *Hillary Clinton wrote a favorable college thesis on Alinsky. Interestingly, when Bill Clinton became president the thesis was locked away. In 1969 she was offered a job with Alinsky's training institute in Chicago. In March 2007, the Washington Post reported that even while in the White House, she continued to give support to Alinsky's Industrial Areas Foundation.*

- *Barack Obama was a student and practitioner of Alinsky's methods. Three of Obama's mentors in Chicago were trained at the Alinsky Industrial Areas Foundation, and for several years Obama taught workshops on the Alinsky method. In 1986, Obama was hired to "organize" residents on the South Side of Chicago. He was also attorney for Association of Community Organizations for Reform Now (ACORN), an organization that emerged out of the Alinsky movement.[31] It is therefore not surprising that he employs Alinsky's radical tactics.*

Another indicator of Obama's true intentions are the last two budgets he submitted to Congress, both of which were overwhelmingly voted down by both houses of Congress. The Senate, acting presumably in concert with Obama, has not passed a budget in three years in violation of the law. The result of this inaction is that the United States continues to race toward financial Armageddon. The following chart, using data from the Congressional Budget Office, shows the problem dramatically.

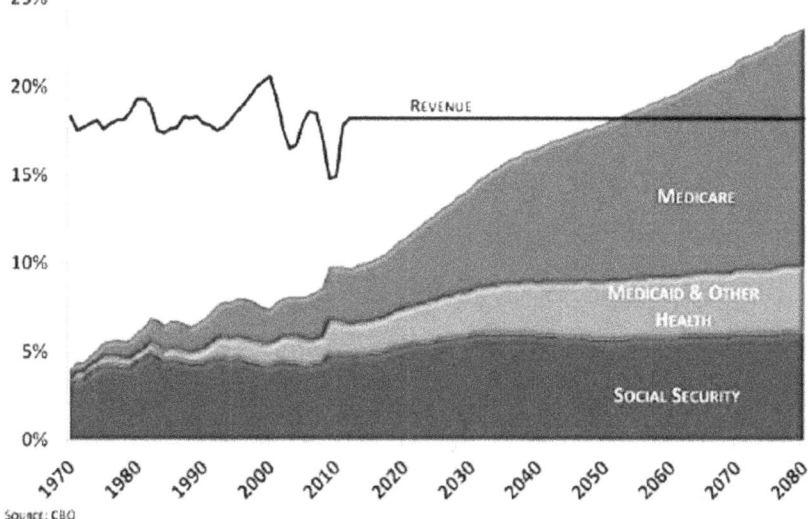

FIGURE 2

WHAT DRIVES OUR DEBT?
(GOVERNMENT SPENDING AS A SHARE OF ECONOMY)

SOURCE: CBO

Considering only the growth in Medicare, Medicaid, and Social Security, the entire amount of annual federal revenue will be consumed by these three programs alone in 40 years. Of course, there will be other spending increases that will shorten the time at which this will happen. Some estimate that we might reach this point in the next two to four years. Even crushing taxes on the rich won't put a dent in this problem. The United States would have to depend on ever more massive borrowing, but we would have no money to pay the interest and no way to pay off the debt. So who in their right mind would lend the United States money?

At that point there would be no money for the military or any other federal departments. Congress would shut down. The executive branch, the federal courts, and the Supreme Court would shut down.

Yet the president and his party sit on their hands and do nothing. What is even worse, they disparage, demagogue, and vote down well-thought-out plans such as the one presented by the House budget committee, *The Path to Prosperity*,[32] which proposes sensible ways to save the country and ensure that the safety-net programs remain viable.

Obama's disregard for this problem and his obsession with ever-increased spending (despite his claims to the contrary) makes one wonder if Obama actually wants this disaster to occur. Of course, if we found ourselves facing such a disaster, we could count on a ruling elite to step forward to save us. Needless to say they would claim supreme power in order to carry out their work. Does this sound a bit familiar?

An *Investor's Business Daily* editorial asked, *Is Obama 'Dangerously Close to Totalitarianism'?*

In the editorial, Judge Andrew Napolitano points out that a few months ago, Obama was saying, "The Congress doesn't count, the Congress doesn't mean anything. I'm going to rule by decree and by administrative regulation." Subsequently, the EPA instigated new rules on coal-fired power plants that in effect stop any future construction of new plants. Obama couldn't get his cap-and-trade legislation enacted by Congress so he simply had one of his agencies, the EPA, create new rules that have the same effect. In another example, his Department of Agriculture was proposing extensive and inane new farm child-labor regulations. This would have severely restricted the things farm kids have traditionally done on the farm. But the real result would be to put the government's fist on farming. Fortunately, there was such an outcry that the proposal was withdrawn—at least until after the 2012 election.

Napolitano states further, "Now he's basically saying the Supreme Court doesn't count. It doesn't matter what they think. They can't review our legislation. That would leave him as the only branch of government standing."

In 2011, a federal district court judge found the Obama interior department in contempt of its ruling that the administration's offshore drilling moratorium was unconstitutional. Subsequently, the department turned around and imposed another moratorium that is essentially the same as the first one.

Obama stated in February 2012, "Whenever Congress refuses to act, [Vice President] Joe [Biden] and I, we're going to act. In the months to come, whenever we have an opportunity, we're going to take steps on our own to keep this economy moving." Congress, the courts, and the Constitution are nuisance to Obama when he doesn't get his way, so he usurps their authority using executive fiat.

The actions of Obama and his administration over more than three years suggest a disturbing pattern. It raises the possibility that Obama may have convictions similar to Lenin and Alinsky. This may or may not be true, but unfortunately the evidence continues to mount.

"Beware of false prophets, which come to you in sheep's clothing, but inwardly they are ravening wolves. Ye shall know them by their fruits" (Matthew 7:15-20).

27 Challenge: Activist Judiciary

Our founding fathers understood the tyranny that comes from power. The whole of human history makes it clear. The colonies understood the importance of working together and that a national government would facilitate this. However, they were very careful to create and enact a constitution and bill of rights designed to strictly limit what the federal government is allowed to do. It was brilliant in how they protected the rights of states to do as they wish and protected the rights of every individual from being transgressed by any level of government.

They also knew there would be disagreements from time to time as to the interpretation and application of the Constitution. For this a federal court system was established with the final arbiter being the Supreme Court. What they probably did not foresee is that some judges and justices would go beyond just interpreting the law but in their rulings actually make new law. This is obviously a violation of the Constitution's separation of powers.

Activist judges dictate these violations on the basis that it is necessary to right a past wrong for "the sake of justice" or "the good of society." What they overlook is an important distinction. The one case where one group can be justifiably favored is when the rights of one party are in conflict with the *rights* of another party. What they must not do is violate the rights of one party to provide a *benefit*, which is not a right, to another party. For example, since education is not a right, it is unjust to give a college admission preference to a group based on race. Why is this so hard to figure out?

Machiavelli was a proponent of achieving ends by any expedient means without regard for the rights of people. He must smile down (or up as the case may be) each time the United States, which prides itself on defending freedom, steps on an individual's rights in the name of some "greater good."

The problem is that there is no one to monitor and control the Supreme Court, which is the final judge. The only recourse is to appoint justices who adhere to the Constitution and make reasonable interpretations of it. And the only way to make this happen is to elect a president and senators who will appoint and confirm this type of justice. And this requires an insightful electorate who vote intelligently.

28 Time for A Makeover

To a large extent, the federal government has become a trillion-dollar-a-year jobs program. As the government has continued to create agencies, rules to be enforced, duplication, and red tape, an ever-growing army of people have been hired to do the work.

The size and complexity of the executive branch has become so vast that the task of trimming it down and making it efficient is overwhelming. Even if there were the will to take it on, conflicting political and personal interests would add an extreme additional level of difficulty.

The enormous growth of the federal government stems primarily from two places—the Sixteenth Amendment, which enacted the federal income tax, and the commerce clause of the Tenth Amendment.

The Constitution gives to the federal government only the specific powers granted to it. Those powers enumerated in the Constitution are for the most part very specific. The commerce clause grants the power to regulate commerce between the states. The intent was to facilitate commerce between the states and keep them from doing things like charging import duties. However, the Supreme Court has interpreted the clause so broadly that it applies to virtually any human activity. As a consequence, Congress and the executive branch have acted without limitation to enact almost anything they have cared to in the name of controlling the country and various social engineering schemes.

The Supreme Court has ruled that ObamaCare is constitutional because the individual mandate in the law is a tax and that the Congress's power to tax is without constitutional limit. This means that the government can force us to buy or do anything by threatening us with a tax if we do not do so.

There is a way out of this if we the people have the will to get our country back. It is a multistep process.

Step 1. Amend the commerce clause so that:

- *Its original intent is clear.*
- *It excludes any activity to the extent that it takes place within a state.*
- *It applies to only the facilitation of buying and selling of tangible products across state lines.*

Step 2. Amend the Constitution to limit the taxing authority of Congress.

Step 3. Develop a plan to remove government agencies and activities that are not allowed under the new amendment. This should be done over time so that states can supplant programs that they consider worthy. In addition, it will allow the reduction in the federal workforce to be absorbed smoothly by the states and private sector.

29 A Final Word

Well, actually a few final words.

Sincere people of sound reasoning and good will, whether liberal or conservative, often have the same goals for the country. Those who are not hooked on the need for power and position should be able to sit down and discuss common objectives and explore the best ways to achieve them. The self-righteous, needy, and greedy need not attend.

Unfortunately, there are some administrations, Congresses, and judges that do not understand why the rights we have by birth and those spelled out in the Constitution are supreme over any goal that is in conflict with them. These people may be well intended, but they want to decide what is best for us at the cost of diminishing our freedom to choose for ourselves. They don't realize that they are ultimately hurting everyone, including those they think they are helping.

Others believe that human rights should not stand in the way of attaining power, changing America into what they think it should be, or obtaining anything else that they want.

The founders of the United States were statesmen, and they were wise. They knew that the rights of the individual are supreme above all else, and that this is the environment in which people and the nation flourish. We should take the challenge to find and elect leaders who can meet this high standard.

If stupidity reigns, as it has so often throughout history, we will suffer the consequences. America is at a tipping point. If we do not elect people who have integrity and a belief in our form of constitutional government, based on the concepts of individual rights and personal responsibility, then our country will fail. It is that serious and will be disastrous for rich and poor alike. But if we have a critical mass of people with the discipline, responsibility, and common sense to elect people who will govern our affairs honestly and logically, then everyone will enjoy growing prosperity. *The choice is ours.*

Appendix A—Testimony of Senator Tom A. Coburn

Committee on Oversight and Government Reform
U.S. House of Representatives
"Government 2.0: GAO Unveils New
Duplicative Program Report"

Tom A. Coburn, M.D. United States Senate Written Testimony

February 28, 2012

Chairman Issa, Ranking Member Cummings, and Members of the Committee:

Thank you for the opportunity to participate in today's hearing on the release of the Government Accountability Office's (GAO) second annual report on duplicative federal programs. Director Dodaro and the staff at GAO are to be commended for their excellent work and dedication to such a large endeavor, one few others in Washington are willing to undertake, but the topic of which is of utmost importance.

Federal duplication and the mismanagement of taxpayer funding in the current labyrinth of government programs is one of the most critical matters currently facing Congress. We must eliminate duplication immediately wherever we find it, and stop making the maze more tangled with our shortsightedness by continuing to create new, unnecessary and duplicative programs. If we do not, Congress will be unable to reign in federal spending and our financial situation will only continue to worsen, while thousands of ineffective government programs continue to fall short of meeting the needs of those we intend to help.

My testimony today will examine some of the primary pitfalls of our current state as a nation of duplication, and provide a look at past and present efforts to eliminate duplication including the comprehensive deficit reduction plan I released last year, and also discuss ways Congress can prevent duplication in the future.

DUPLICATION NATION

The findings of GAO's 2012 report, as detailed by Director Dodaro, are a sobering reminder and a revealing look at a government grown far beyond what many imagined possible, funding hundreds of programs decidedly outside the scope of the Enumerated Powers as enshrined in the Constitution. And like last year's report, which identified more than $100 billion in budgetary savings by simply eliminating duplicative programs, today's findings are a testament to failed congressional efforts of oversight and a reminder Congress continue to shirk its duty to address even blatant areas of waste and mismanagement of taxpayer funding.

Not one corner of our daily life remains untouched by a government program or federal effort. From what we eat and drink, to where we live, work, and socialize, nearly every aspect of human behavior and American society are addressed by multiple government programs. Nearly every federal agency runs a program overlapping with a handful of other programs across several additional agencies. Whether carrying out similar missions or funding similar projects, everything the government is doing once it is likely doing twice or three times and often not very well.

In just a few examples from last year's report,[1] nearly 430 programs are listed as part of extensive duplication across dozens of agencies.

Though some view this permeation of government as success, its enormity may actually now work against original intentions and instead keep those who need the help from finding it. In their 2011 duplication report, GAO noted, —This fragmentation can create difficulties for people in accessing services as well as administrative burdens for providers who must navigate various application requirements. GAO went on to explain, the lack of coordination caused by duplication poses a barrier to the delivery of services to those in need.[2]

Consider, the entirety of federal programs cannot even be compiled in a list for review. No one single inventory of all federal programs exists. Those in Congress tasked with reviewing these programs, since they refuse to do it themselves, cannot even do so in one year's time. Federal agencies and departments have proven themselves incapable of providing a full account of each program in their own jurisdiction.

Who is to blame for this maze of government programs? Very simply, it is Congress. We are all culpable. And to be sure, the blame does not rest on one party or the other, it lies with both. Duplication in this country has been created by the ruling class of career politicians seeking to slap short-term fixes on problems in order to claim credit at home and recognition in Washington.

Though the Executive Branch is not without fault, Congress is the main offender. We set the budget, we pass the appropriations bills and we authorize new activities at the federal agencies. We refuse to apply metrics and standards to the programs we create. We ignore our duty to conduct oversight. And we choose to remain uninformed about existing efforts before creating new ones. Despite the thousands of existing federal programs on the books, nearly every passing week Congress creates more programs and federal efforts, piling new initiatives on top of the old ones, which were created on top of even older programs.

In an often frantic effort to claim credit for addressing the latest social or economic problem of the day, members of Congress propose and pass legislation, while the president signs into law, new programs and even new federal agencies, duplicating existing efforts, few of which can be shown to demonstrate any measurable results. For example, Congress recently rushed to pass the Dodd-Frank financial regulatory legislation, which created three new federal entities, the Financial Stability Oversight Council, the Office of Financial Research, and the Bureau of Consumer Financial Protection. Yet, in January 2009, GAO described the already extensive federal financial regulatory system as fragmented and complex, and ill-suited to meet the nation's needs in the 21st century, stating, Today, responsibilities for overseeing the financial services industry are shared among almost a dozen federal banking, securities, futures, and other regulatory agencies, numerous self-regulatory organizations, and hundreds of state financial regulatory agencies.[3]

A 1966 *Nation's Business* article outlined the issue clearly, and more than four decades later, the problem remains.

Any organization that spends more than $140 billion a year as the federal government does....is certain to have confusion, duplication, and waste in its operation. There is no large private enterprise which does not have some of the same. However, the volume of duplication and confusion in federal ranks has now grown so large that even those who claim liberal attitudes toward both big government and centralized superplanning swallow hard at the thought of it all. Scores of others departments, agencies, programs, plans and projects were created either by Congress acting on its own, under White House pressure or through that misty process by which bureaucrats expand and multiply their jobs, their paper work, their agencies and even multiply themselves. [4]

Not only is the web of government programs placing an enormous strain on taxpayers, and likely reducing the effectiveness of the delivery of many services, it is so interwoven and completely unmanageable, that the goals of many programs now stand in direct contradiction to each other.

Take for example, something as simple as potato chips. The government, namely Congress and the Executive Branch, cannot decide if they like them or not, if fried potatoes are healthy, if we should eat them or if they should be banned, or if instead, we should spend money promoting the chip industry. In their first report on duplication, the GAO found the federal government spent more than $62.5 billion on 18 domestic food and nutrition assistance programs in fiscal year 2008. [5] While many of these programs, such as the Supplemental Nutrition Assistance Program (SNAP) allow federal funds to purchase potato chips, dozens of other government wide initiatives, are aimed at keeping Americans healthy, specifically suggesting food like potato chips should be limited in intake, and perhaps even taken out of public schools all together. At the same time, just this year the Department of Agriculture announced a nearly $50,000 federal grant was being doled out to a private potato chip company in New York. According to the proposal, this money would be used to overhaul their media strategy and raise brand awareness and consumer knowledge essentially encouraging people to buy and consume potato chips![6] Meanwhile, potato chips sales in the United States alone exceed $6 billion annually,[7] which begs the question why the taxpayers are now asked to subsidize promotion and marketing for the industry.

The effectiveness of the existing myriad of government programs can scarcely be demonstrated, while Congress refuses to conduct oversight of existing efforts, piling layers upon layers of costly, unneeded bureaucracy. Meanwhile, taxpayers are paying for duplication, contradiction, and getting little in return except confusion, a trillion dollar deficit, and if we do not fix it soon, likely higher taxes in the future.

[1] Government Accountability Office, *Opportunities to Reduce Potential Duplication in Government Programs, Save Tax Dollars, and Enhance Revenue*, March 2001, GAO-11-318SP, http://www.gao.gov/assets/320/315920.pdf

[2] Government Accountability Office, *Opportunities to Reduce Potential Duplication in Government Programs, Save Tax Dollars, and Enhance Revenue*, March 2001, GAO-11-318SP, http://www.gao.gov/assets/320/315920.pdf

[3] Government Accountability Office, *Financial Regulation: A Framework for Crafting and Assessing Proposals to Modernize the Outdated U.S. Financial Regulatory System*, January 2009, GAO-09-216, http://www.gao.gov/new.items/d09216.pdf

[4]—Government by Totem Pole, *Nation's Business*, October 1966

[5] Government Accountability Office, *Opportunities to Reduce Potential Duplication in Government Programs, Save Tax Dollars, and Enhance Revenue*, March 2001, GAO-11-318SP, http://www.gao.gov/assets/320/315920.pdf

ELIMINATING DUPLICATION: LOOKING BACK

Proposals to address duplication are not a new trend in Washington. This of course means duplication in the beltway bureaucracy is not new either. Over the course of more than 100 years, Washington has created thousands of government programs, hundreds of which overlap hundreds more. Duplication is a longstanding federal issue, and along the way, many have tried to raise the warning sign. Numerous efforts have been launched by both members of Congress and presidents to eliminate duplicative government programs, and prevent the problem from multiplying, in hopes Washington could stop itself before the problem grew out of control.

Even in 1905, some in Washington recognized government's bent toward duplication and mismanagement of taxpayer dollars. That year, *the San Francisco Chronicle* editorialized, It is in the superabundance of officials, the duplication of work growing out of the squabbles of the bureaus and departments, unnecessary travelling and printing, luxurious equipment and the like. No possible retrenchment in this direction will extinguish the deficit, but it can reduce it by some millions.[8]

By 1909, the Senate Budget Committee adopted a resolution to investigate the business methods observed   by executive branch agencies because of a lack of cooperation, duplication of work,   by agencies and independent agencies which costs hundreds of thousands a year.[9]

Less than ten years later, in 1920, a group of senators started a war on duplicative spending in the federal government with the intent to cut through the entanglements of red tape, the outer defense of the bureaucrat and his battalions of pencil-pushers and typewriters to put the United States Government, with its war debts of more than $20,000,000,000 on a businesslike basis.[10] At the time, the *New York Times* opined on the topic noting in 1920, The cynics at the national capital laugh and say that all attempts to make genuine reform in Congress and in the departments will fail as they have in the past. But many men of reputed wisdom predict that Congress, now at a low ebb in the esteem of the people, must at last act with deep-cutting thoroughness to regain a position of respect.[11]

Even presidents were involved in the effort, and in 1925, President Calvin Coolidge initiated an investigation of government red tape and duplication of effort in the smaller departments of the federal government.[12]

In 1950, Senator Styles Bridges designed an eight-point proposal to cut $6 billion from the federal budget. Senator Bridges included a proposal to abandon creating new programs until we could afford them, and also to eliminate duplication from the federal budget. Meanwhile, the Joint Committee on Reduction of Non-Essential Federal Expenditures found that 37 agencies were conducting activities related to public health, 64 in business relations and 24 in mapmaking.[13]

In his book With No Apologies, former Senator Barry Goldwater detailed one account of duplication discovered during the Roth investigation. Congressman William Roth, a young member from Delaware had spent two years trying to determining how many public assistance programs were available in the federal establishment. He found there were 1,300 programs administered by a variety of agencies. They operated separately. There was no communication in between them, and they were unknown to many of the people they were established to help.[14]

In the 1970s, Senator Edmund Muskie of Maine explained the proliferation of federal programs, accompanied by duplication and inefficiencies had created a bumper crop of public disenchantment with government so unresponsive that it cannot even perform simple day-to-day tasks that need to be done. He pointed out in 1975 the government listed 1,030 aid programs (including 228 for health) and 1,249 advisory boards, committees, commissions and councils[15] Current Secretary of Defense, Leon Panetta, acknowledged in 1997 the prolific duplication that exists in our government, including the Defense Department, which as today's GAO report clearly outlines, little has changed 15 years later. Sometimes, in all the confusion about budgeting, programs that have become inefficient or simply irrelevant get rubber-stamped, surviving many years beyond their usefulness. The waste and duplication show up in civilian and military programs alike, and for the citizen it boils down to more red tape – and more taxes.[16]

[6] Press Release, Office of Senator Gillibrand, —Gillibrand Announces Nearly $50,000 in Value-Added Producer Grant for Long Island Farm, February 8, 2012, http://www.gillibrand.senate.gov/newsroom/press/release/gillibrand-announces-nearly50000-in-value-added-producer-grant-for-long-island-farm

[7] Snack Food Association, A Century and a Half of Crunch: The Potato Chip Turns 150!, http://www.sfa.org/potato150.aspx

[8] Editorial, —Economical Administration: The President's Task on Overhauling the Government Departments, San Francisco Chronicle, June 28, 1905

[9] O'Laughlin, John Callan, —Committee Seeks Federal Economy: Senate Body Will Investigate Departments to End Useless Expense, Chicago Tribune, June 5, 2009

[10]Tiller, Theodore, Congress Starts Drive on Waste in Governmental Departments, Baltimore Sun, April 18, 1920.

[11] —Will Congress Stop Federal Wastefulness? New York Times, March 14, 1920

[12] To Investigate Government Red Tape, Wall Street Journal, April 10, 1925

[13] Bridge Proposes Slash in Spending: Offers an 8-Point Program for Cutting $6,000,000,000 From Appropriations,|| New York Times, May 16, 1950

[14] Barry Goldwater, With No Apologizes, The Personal and Political Memoirs of United States Senator Barry Goldwater,

[15] How to leash runaway U.S. Programs, the Christian Science Monitor, May 17, 1976

[16] Panetta, Leon E, A Blueprint for Fiscal Disaster Los Angeles Times, December 6, 1997

ELIMINATING DUPLICATION: TODAY IN WASHINGTON

Though these examples remind us duplication has long been a problem in the Washington bureaucracy, we have little to show in the win column when it comes to specifically addressing and eliminating duplication. Throughout history, these efforts have continually been met with opposition from career politicians, congressional staff and lobbyists, and defenders of special interests entrenched in a culture that screams Washington knows best and places personal ambition and comfort above doing what is right for the country.

Even today, we're witnessing the same. The second report released today by GAO is a report card, outlining what Congress and this administration have and have not done to address the dozens of areas of duplication GAO exposed last year. While no one in Washington is without fault, Congress has done virtually nothing to implement the 176 specific recommendations included in last year's report. In nearly half of the areas listed as requiring congressional action, Congress has done nothing. Of the 81 general areas reviewed in the report, only four have been completely addressed by Congress and the president, while 17 have not been addressed in any way GAO could identify.

For example, the 2011 GAO report outlined there are more than 173 tax expenditures, many of which have related mission areas to spending programs in the discretionary budget. Yet, Congress continues to ignore tax reform, refuses to eliminate any duplicative tax credits, and instead is set to extend them once again, at a cost of hundreds of billions of dollars.

Even though the current administration has not done enough to address duplication, they are taking steps to propose eliminations and consolidations, and have done so with little help from Congress. In fact, their efforts to simply propose a draft framework for consolidating the six primary departments and agencies focused on business and trade in the federal government were met with opposition in Congress. It is clear they will have little help from those in Congress with jurisdiction over these programs, who instead are waging a turf war and holding tight to their parochial interests.

Despite an overall lack of interest or action by Congress to address last year's duplication findings, one notable and promising exception, worth highlighting today, is legislation introduced in December by Rep. Virginia Foxx (R-NC), chairwoman of the Subcommittee on Higher Education and Workforce Training.

A year ago, the GAO identified a sprawl of federal job training and employment programs that only politicians and government bureaucrats could dream up. GAO found 47 federal job training programs, with separate administrative structures, costing $18 billion annually. All but three programs were found to duplicate at least one other program, providing similar services to similar populations.

Given the dearth of meaningful program evaluations, GAO found little is known about the effectiveness of these programs. Only five of the 47 programs have had an impact study since 2004, and only half have had a program evaluation. What's more, GAO identified another 51 programs that potentially could have been identified as job training programs but failed to meet GAOs narrow definition of a program. For example, the Social Security Administration's Ticket to Work program was not considered by GAO to be a job training and employment program.

A year after publication of this report, Congress has not acted to meaningfully consolidate programs and has all but ignored GAOs findings. However, Chairwoman Foxx introduced the *Streamlining*

Workforce Development Programs Act (H.R. 3610), legislation that consolidates 33 of the 47 job training programs identified in GAO's 2011 report. This legislation also seeks to increase accountability of the programs and create an outcome driven job training system. I am wholeheartedly in support of her effort, and grateful for the work she has done in this area. Now, it is Congress' job to finish this work and pass this legislation, and put it on the president's desk to be signed.

Even more, it is time for the rest of Congress, and every congressional committee to do the same. Every committee must begin addressing the areas of duplication in their jurisdiction and putting forth creative and commonsense proposals to consolidate, streamline, eliminate, downsize, and make the government more efficient. It is time to do more with less, not less with more.

BACK IN BLACK: A $9 TRILLION DEFICIT REDUCTION PLAN

As part of my own efforts to address duplication throughout the federal budget, in July 2011, I released _Back in Black_, a comprehensive deficit reduction plan scrutinizing every corner of the federal budget for savings.[17] _Back in Black_ listed hundreds of specific proposals which together would eliminate more than $9 trillion of deficit spending over ten years.

Back in Black was the culmination of many years of work in my office that began with smaller iterations of lists of government waste, mismanagement and duplication, divided by agency. I remained unsatisfied with answers received when requesting lists of federal programs for purposes of determining duplication, and disappointed there was not a single depository for areas of potential savings to taxpayers from elimination of waste and duplication. At the same time, my staff had for years, on a daily basis, found examples of waste and duplication at nearly every single federal agency. Compiling this information into a comprehensive look at the government would give us a full picture of just exactly how bad the mess is Washington has created. As such, this summer I asked my staff to dedicate six weeks to compiling everything we had on every government program, office, task force, commission, entitlement program, agency and department.

The result was a 622-page document with hundreds of specific recommendations for savings, based on our findings of rampant duplication, mismanagement, fraud, and waste throughout every single government entity. Beginning with discretionary spending, the plan calls for $4 trillion over ten years in savings from this portion of the budget, with no department left untouched, from the Defense Department to the Congress and the White House, and every agency in-between. In addition, *Back in Black* includes detailed proposals reforming Medicare and Medicaid to save $2.6 trillion over ten years, while also reforming Social Security, making it fully solvent for the next 75 years. *Back in Black* also makes a large down payment on comprehensive tax reform with a thorough examination of the tax code. The plan calls for eliminating and reforming more than more 40 tax credits and deductions, many of which are little more than socialist spending programs masquerading as tax cuts that allow certain groups and companies to pay lower taxes simply because they are well-connected in Washington. If all of these reductions and reforms are implemented, federal borrowing will decrease dramatically, saving taxpayers an additional $1.3 trillion in interest payments on the national debt.

Instead of relying on arbitrary across-the-board reductions in spending, which show little deference to programs that may be working and do little to target spending to those in need, the approach of *Back in Black* was meant to be thoughtful, comprehensive, and hopefully a path toward compromise, that left no sacred cow of Washington un-tipped, as it looked at the Defense budget, the tax code, Social Security, and every other corner of the budget. As stated in the first pages of *Back in Black*, This plan recognizes all spending is not created equal by asking those with more to take less to ensure those who gave more will not be left with nothing. It ensures health care for wounded combat veterans, while ending unemployment benefits for jobless millionaires.[18]

I set out to find the most commonsense places for reductions and eliminations, hoping to make the case based on evidenced waste, fraud, and duplication, that members of Congress on both sides could not deny, but instead would join together to eliminate.

Many of the proposals in *Back in Black* are closely intertwined with GAO findings, as well as our own, on duplication throughout the Washington bureaucracy. In fact, the word duplicate is found 322 times throughout the plan. In every agency, in every section of the report, we found and compiled hundreds of examples of duplication, including many from the GAO report. The more we dug, the more we found. Every single agency is participating in nearly every activity one could imagine. Eradicating duplication was a large part of the savings found throughout *Back in Black*, and the plan assumed a conservative estimate of $50 billion in savings over ten years from addressing duplication in many different areas including job training, economic development, STEM programs, financial literacy, housing assistance, Department of Justice programs, Homeland Security grants and dozens more.[19]

I understand few may agree with every single recommendation of *Back in Black*. But, if on a list with hundreds of ideas, we could find even half on which to agree, then Congress would be $4.5 trillion further along in addressing our country's debilitating deficit and rising debt.

[17] Office of Senator Tom Coburn, *Back in Black*, June 2011, http://1.usa.gov/qCwHD8

Examples of Proposals in *Back in Black*

Eliminate Sweet Heart Deals for Government Contractors

Savings: At least $2 billion over ten years

Collect Unpaid Taxes Owed by Federal Employees

Savings: $1 billion over ten years

Reduce Congress' Spending on Itself

Savings: $3.82 billion over ten years

Stop Overpaying Drug Companies

Savings: $480 million over ten years

End Unemployment Payments to Millionaires

Savings: $186 million over ten years

Reduce Advertising by the Federal Government

Savings: $5.6 billion over ten years

Use Better Measure of Inflation to Determine Increases in Benefit Payments

Savings: Approximately $180 billion over ten years

End Payments for Coal Cleanup When Projects Have Been Certified as Being Completed

Savings: $1.23 billion over ten years

Get the Department of Defense Out of Education and the Grocery Store Business

Savings: $19 billion over ten years

Terminate HHS's Community Economic Development Program

Savings: $38 million over ten years.

End Federal Subsidies to Wealthy Doctors and Hospitals for Health Information Technology

Savings: $15.6 billion over ten years.

Stop Medicare Payments for Uncovered Services

Savings: $1.97 billion over ten years.

[18] Office of Senator Tom Coburn, *Back in Black*, June 2011, http://1.usa.gov/qCwHD8

[19] Appendix A includes a series of charts summarizing the overall recommendations in Back in Black, as well as highlights of proposals from several specific areas of concentration.

PREVENTING FUTURE DUPLICATION

Since release of GAO's first report on duplication, the Senate has twice rejected bipartisan legislation aimed at preventing future duplication.

The amendment would require for every bill before consideration in the Senate:

- *an analysis by the Congressional Research Service (CRS) to determine if the bill creates any new federal program, office, or initiative that would duplicate or overlap any existing federal program, office, or initiative with similar mission, purpose, goals, or activities;*
- *a listing of all of the overlapping or duplicative federal program or programs, office or offices, or initiative or initiatives; and*
- *an explanation provided by the committee as to why the creation of each new program, office, or initiative is necessary if a similar program or programs, office or offices, or initiative or initiatives already exist.*

This CRS duplication score, similar to a Congressional Budget Office cost analysis also required before congressional consideration, would serve as a tool to further inform members and the public of the impact and ramifications of a bill.

The measure received 64 votes in June of last year, but fell three votes shy of the 67 votes required for passage of any change to Senate rules.[20] The Senate voted on the measure a second time this year, and again, it failed to garner the votes necessary for passage.[21]

I plan to offer this amendment to every moving vehicle considered in the Senate until it is accepted. The House should also immediately pass similar legislation requiring a rules change to provide for a CRS duplication score on any legislation before consideration in the House.

Requiring a duplication score before Congress votes on legislation, will help guard against our own worst tendencies, ensuring full knowledge and disclosure when duplicative programs are created in the future.

Further, members of Congress should begin to find government waste and duplication in their own states and bring it to light. In July 2011, I released a 41-page report detailing 30 specific programs and projects funded by the federal government within my own state of Oklahoma, costing taxpayers at least $170 million.[22] The Oklahoma Waste Report: Exposing Washington's Wasteful Spending Habits in our Own Backyard exposed several areas of government duplication, in Oklahoma, including state grant awards from duplicative Department of Agriculture programs assisting in the development of farmers' markets, and more than $1 million in FY 2010 from the duplicative Resource Conservation and Development program, which was targeted for elimination by both President Obama and President Bush alike. I strongly encourage members of Congress to bring to light examples of duplication from their own states, and use this as a foundation to consolidated overlapping federal efforts.

[20] 112 Congress, 1st Session, Senate Roll Call Vote #102, June 29, 2011, S. Amdt. 521 to S. Res. 116,

http://www.senate.gov/legislative/LIS/roll_call_lists/roll_call_vote_cfm.cfm?congress=112&session=1&vote=00102

[21] 112 Congress, 2Session, Senate Roll Call Vote #10, February 2, 2012, S.Amdt. 1473 to S. Amdt. 1470 to S. 2038,

http://www.senate.gov/legislative/LIS/roll_call_lists/roll_call_vote_cfm.cfm?congress=112&session=2&vote=00010

GAO'S REPORT ON DUPLICATION: THE PATH FORWARD

With the release of today's GAO report, combined with last year's recommendations, Congress and the administration have been given extensive details in 132 areas of government duplication and opportunities for significant cost savings, with dozens of recommendations for how to address the duplication and find these savings.

The problem in Congress today is not an issue of ignorance—it is one of indifference and incompetence. We know we have a problem. We know we have cancer. Yet, we refuse to stop making it worse, we refuse to apply the treatment, and we refuse to take the pain of the medication for the long-term benefit of a cure.

The GAO report released today provides a very clear and concise listing of dozens of areas ripe for reform and in need of collaboration from members on both sides of the aisle, to find solutions to address these issues. And yet, the second GAO report released today, our report card, demonstrates the clear unwillingness of Congress to do any work to address duplication, even when the information, background, and even specific recommendations, are delivered directly to our door.

It was said last year by both Republicans and Democrats that GAO's first report on duplication would serve as a roadmap for extensive federal savings, to help put us on a path of fiscal solvency and begin reducing our deficit. These pledges were quickly set aside, and exchanged for partisan bickering and a refusal to find even the simplest areas of commonality.

We are looking into a future of trillion dollar deficits and a national debt quickly headed toward $20 trillion. Our nation is not on the verge of bankruptcy—it is already bankrupt. We have maxed out our own credit cards and are now living off our children's credit

cards, while funding a government with so many duplicative programs they cannot even all be written down in a more than 420
page report.

Over the last two years, there have been countless discussion
and bipartisan talks about how to address our debt and deficit, turn
our country around, and get the economy back on its feet and growing. Yet, there has been little agreement, and at the end of this year
we will be faced with another tax extenders package and another
increase in the debt limit, all while sequestration will be poised to
kick in and achieve the savings Congress has been unable to muster
the courage to pass.

But, before us today, we have part of the answer. GAO's work
presents Washington with literally hundreds of options for areas in
which we could make a decision now to start finding savings, potentially hundreds of billions of dollars. If we, as members of Congress,
are unable to agree on eliminating even one small duplicative program or tax credit, when clearly we know there are hundreds, we
have little hope of ever coming to a comprehensive compromise for
fixing our floundering budget.

How many more housing programs do we need before we have
solved the homeless problem? How many food assistance programs
do we need to ensure the hungry are fed? How many education
programs do we need to improve our schools? Ten? Twenty? Hundreds? Just remember, next time someone in Congress proposes a
bill to create a new program to address a problem, ask yourself, are

we not addressing this problem already? Instead of creating a new program, we must demand results from the ones that already exist.

For the sake of our future as a nation, in the coming days and weeks, as we once again hear similar promises from Washington to address the issues exposed by GAO today, I can only hope Congress will this time work together to implement these recommendations and heed the advice found in the pages of this report.

[22] Office of Senator Tom Coburn, —Oklahoma Waste Report: Exposing Washington's Wasteful Spending Habits in our Own Backyard,|| July 2011, http://www.coburn.senate.gov/public/index. cfm?a=Files.Serve&File_id=4f875398-b8bd-4fff-a37a2cfe984bc3ec

Appendix B—Back In Black Highlights

BACK IN BLACK: A DEFICIT REDUCTION PLAN HIGHLIGHTS

Office of Senator Tom Coburn

All savings are over ten years unless otherwise noted

GENERAL GOVERNMENT – SAVINGS: $974.1 BILLION (MANDATORY: $62.5 BILLION, DISCRETIONARY: $911.5 BILLION)
Key points:

❖ Sets a good example for the rest of the country by reducing and eliminating general government excess spending.

❖ Shows that Washington is serious and willing to make sacrifices to save our country.

❖ Support the President's efforts to reform federal IT management and close duplicative federal government data centers.

Recommendations:

➢ Reduces the number of limos owned by federal agencies. Savings: $10.4 million a year

➢ Eliminates agency Hollywood liaison offices. Savings: $3.2 million a year

➢ Reduces agency travel, advertising, printing, and conferences budgets: $4.9 billion a year

CONGRESS – SAVINGS: $4.3 BILLION
Key point:

❖ It is time for serious leadership, which should begin by Congress significantly cutting its own budget by 15 percent and eliminating wasteful spending.

Recommendations & examples:

➢ Reduce the Senate and House of Representatives accounts by 15 percent: $3.8 billion

➢ Freeze pay for Members of Congress for three years: $6 million

➤ Achieve savings by reducing printing costs of congressional documents: $312.28 million

EXECUTIVE OFFICE OF THE PRESIDENT – SAVINGS: $5.4 BILLION
Key points:

❖ With a budget of nearly $830 million, the Executive Office of the President (EOP) funds the day-to-day functions of the White House. While President Obama proposed a 3.5 percent cut for his White House budget in 2012, this time of record deficits calls for bolder measures.

❖ This plan adopts the recommendation of the President's National Commission on Fiscal Responsibility and Reform, which proposed a 15 percent reduction in the White House budget.

Recommendations:

➤ Eliminate the Office of National Drug Control Policy (ONDCP) - $4.7 billion

➤ Eliminate the Council of Environmental Quality (CEQ) - $33 million

➤ Eliminate the Office of Science and Technology Policy (OSTP) - $77 million

DEPARTMENT OF AGRICULTURE – SAVINGS: $346.40 BILLION
Key points

❖ Farm safety net programs are modernized to reflect the strength of American agriculture and advances in modern farming while ensuring farmers are well capitalized.

❖ The structure and integrity of important domestic nutrition assistance payments are enhanced to ensure those who continue to be impacted by our nation's struggling economy have access to healthy food.

❖ U.S. charities are provided more autonomy in their operations by removing inefficient federal financing methods for international food aid.

Recommendations & examples:

➤ Ends duplicative market export programs that fund profitable companies and large trade associations. Savings: $2 billion.

➤ Reduces the Rural Development agency's funding for non-rural or non-economically distressed recipients, such as $54 million for the Mohegan Sun Casino, $2.5 million for a Smithsonian style country music museum, and various grants to wineries and breweries. Savings: $26.9 billion.

➤ Ends payments to private landowners for allowing individuals to access their land for hunting, fishing, bird watching and other recreational activities that landowners are financially incentivized to offer without federal support. Savings: $555 million.

DEPARTMENT OF COMMERCE – SAVINGS: $26.84 BILLION
Key points:

❖ Important programs within DOC are consolidated with similar programs in the federal government to reduce duplication and costs.

❖ The U.S. Patent and Trademark Office is freed to operate more effectively and efficiently to benefit the inventors who actually pay to use the system.

❖ Americans will have the opportunity to fill out the next Census online, saving themselves time and tax revenue.

❖ Marine conservation and protection programs within NOAA are transferred to the Department of Interior (DOI), to increase the effectiveness of these programs and similar programs within DOI.

❖ Trade enforcement and export promotion efforts are streamlined into one agency, which will serve as a one-stop shop for all businesses looking for export assistance and enable more focused trade enforcement action by our government.

Recommendations & examples:

➤ Ends NOAA's management of two weather satellite systems that have incurred cost overruns of more than $7.5 billion (a 59 percent cost overrun) even though the amount of satellites being purchased has been reduced. Resulting savings are $2.2 billion.

➤ Ends a taxpayer subsidized business consulting program that costs taxpayers $125 million annually, resulting in $1.25 billion in savings.

➤ Eliminates billions of dollars in taxpayer liability in government-backed investments in other countries.

➤ Ends taxpayer support for a duplicative agency that is seen as a Congressional "Cookie Jar" for special projects and relies on self-reported data from the recipients of funding to determine the effectiveness of the program. This saves taxpayers $2.93 billion.

➤ Eliminates a program that has been used as a slush fund for NOAA instead of for seafood promotion efforts. Resulting savings are $1.05 billion.

DEPARTMENT OF DEFENSE – SAVINGS: $1.006 TRILLION (DISCRETIONARY: $963.3 BILLION, MANDATORY: $43 BILLION)
Key points:

❖ Reduces spending at the Defense Department on lower priority programs but makes no reductions or estimates regarding combat operations in Afghanistan or Iraq.

❖ Gets Pentagon out of nondefense missions such as grocery stores, schools and duplicative medical research.

❖ Reforms and modernizes military health care for retired veterans that were not injured by their military service.

❖ Adopts certain Fiscal Commission recommendations on weapon systems, troop levels, and military personnel reforms.

DEPARTMENT OF EDUCATION – SAVINGS: $409.10 BILLION
Key points:

❖ Removes the federal government's role in the public school system, returning complete authority over education to state and local school districts.

❖ Contains costs of the Pell Grant program while protecting the program features that have made Pell Grants successful.

❖ Saves much needed room on the federal balance sheets by shifting the student loan program exclusively to the private sector where it belongs.

Recommendations & examples:

➤ Saves state and local education systems millions of dollars they spend each year complying with requirements of the Elementary and Secondary Education Act. States and school districts work 7.8 million hours each year collecting and disseminating information required under Title I of federal education law, and those hours cost more than $235 million.

➤ Prevents the Department of Education from becoming one of the world's largest banks by getting bureaucrats out of the student loan business.

➤ Ends the mandatory portion of the Pell Grant program which is helping to drive up program costs, **saving $78.3 billion**.

DEPARTMENT OF ENERGY – SAVINGS: $101.77 BILLION
Key points:

❖ U.S. energy security is prioritized by targeting DOE's focus on advancing the production of domestic natural resources.

❖ DOE programs are streamlined to ensure it operates at peak efficiency without overlap of private ventures.

❖ The questions surrounding nuclear power are answered by providing direction for the future of nuclear spent fuel that allows states or private entities the option of taking on waste storage responsibilities.

Recommendations & examples:

➤ Reduces funding for the 900 conferences and symposia held where taxpayer dollars were spent on entertaining guests at yacht clubs with extravagant meals, cigars, and wine. Savings: over $428 million.

➤ Ends ineffective appliance labeling program found riddled with fraud, leading consumers to believe they were purchasing efficient products. **Savings: $627 million.**

➤ Ends duplicative weatherization program that was found to be poorly managed. **Savings: $2 billion.**

DEPARTMENT OF HEALTH & HUMAN SERVICES - SAVINGS: $106.70 BILLION (Mandatory) Key point:

❖ To help prevent waste, fraud, and abuse in Medicare and Medicaid, more resources need to be focused in an aggressive timeline to

Recommendations:

- ➢ Replace outdated technology systems with cutting-edge technologies;
- ➢ Foster a cooperative culture of data-sharing and timely analysis in public-private partnerships;
- ➢ Encourage the widespread adoption of industry standards;
- ➢ Incentivize the identification and prosecution of waste, fraud, and abuse;
- ➢ Better monitor and enforce drug policies to curb overutilization and abuse;
- ➢ Better protect beneficiary and provider identification numbers from being defrauded by implementing safeguards;
- ➢ Increase penalties for the theft and resale of beneficiary and provider identification numbers;
- ➢ Leverage a range of technologies to examine payments and billing patterns before reimbursement claims are paid,
- ➢ Reform CMS management of its program integrity contractors by increasing accountability and oversight, and;
- ➢ Adopt transformative coverage and payment models with proven records of lower costs, better care, and reduced levels of abuse and fraud.

(Discretionary) Key points:

❖ Repeals the worst parts of the *Affordable Care Act* and other federal programs that dictate the practice of medicine and interfere with the patient-physician relationship.

❖ Prioritizes funding for basic research and life-saving drugs instead of wasteful programs that don't deliver results and are run by organizations propped up on government grants.

❖ Annual funding increases in medical research at NIH continue.

MEDICARE & MEDICAID SAVINGS: $2.64 TRILLION THE DEPARTMENT OF HOUSING AND URBAN DE- VELOPMENT – SAVINGS: $88.73 BILLION
Key point:

❖ Improves living conditions of public housing and ensures federal aid benefits the needy rather than the greedy by evicting slum lords.

Recommendations:

➢ Directing More Resources to Housing Assistance by Consolidating Duplicative Programs.

➢ Ending Federal Housing Payments to Slum Lords.

➢ Prohibiting the Repayment of HUD Loans with HUD Grants.

➢ Preventing Bailouts of Risky Government-backed Mortgages. Ex) bailouts of Fannie Mae and Freddie Mac are estimated to cost taxpayers $317 billion.

➢ Eliminating Unnecessary, Inefficient, and Wasteful Programs. Ex) eliminating the Brownfields Economic Development Initiative (BEDI), that is duplicative of state government efforts, would save $18 million a year.

➢ Requiring Modest Rent Contributions of Tenants Receiving Housing Assistance. CBO projects this reform would save a total of $26.4 billion.

➢ Reducing Excessive Overhead Costs and Unnecessary Bureaucracy. HUD spends approximately $537 million on salaries and expenses for administration, operations and management, including funds for advertising and promotional activities. This amount should be reduced by 15 percent, which would be a savings of $80 million.

➢ Directing AIDS Housing to Those with the Greatest Need. Over the past decade, scandals involving tens of millions of dollars of misspent federal AIDS housing have come to light across the country.

Examples of waste:

➤ HUD awards hundreds of millions of dollars to slum lords for dangerous and unsanitary housing.

➤ HUD pays the rent of hundreds of dead people.

➤ HUD's largest affordable housing block grant program squandered $650 million on over 1,000 stalled or abandoned projects.

➤ HUD has lost 39 cents on the dollar for every home it resold

➤ A wealthy international architecture firm, a "doggie day care," and upgrades to Victorian cottages among the recipients of HUD community development program that steers millions of dollars to dubious projects.

DEPARTMENT OF THE INTERIOR – SAVINGS: $26.44 BILLION
Key points:

❖ President Obama's recommendations for administrative efficiency and lower overhead are adopted, ensuring greater efficiency and focus on the constituencies served.

❖ The urgent multi-billion dollar maintenance needs of the nation's public lands and our greatest national treasures are made priorities, while eliminating non-essential grant programs and unsustainable land purchases.

❖ Prevention of destructive wildfires is prioritized by consolidating duplicative wildland fire management programs and allowing greater focus on effective, proven prevention strategies.

❖ Core resource protection programs that preserve and enhance our national parks are preserved and prioritized, while scaling back on non-essential social science and duplicative outside research programs.

Recommendations & examples:

➢ Ends hundreds of millions of dollars in coal cleanup payments to states and tribes who have long completed cleanup efforts. **Saves $1.23 billion.**

➢ Prohibits funding for next phase of renovations on the Department of the Interior's "limestone and granite clad" headquarters in Washington, D.C. The makeover has now lasted a decade, with more years and millions of dollars more planned. (Administration request for FY 2012- $50.4 million)

DEPARTMENT OF JUSTICE – SAVINGS: $34.54 BILLION
Key points:

❖ The fundamental mission of the Department of Justice is pre-served, and the department will continue to vigorously pros-ecute federal criminals and defend the United States in court.

❖ Eliminates overlap and duplication among DOJ programs and ends those that clearly are not working to ensure effective pro-grams are properly managed.

❖ Frees the states to make their own decisions when it comes to criminal justice policy by releasing them from the burdensome requirements of federal funding.

Recommendations & examples:

➤ Ends the Parole Commission, which was eliminated by Con-gress along with federal parole in 1984. **Savings: $12.9 million per year.**

➤ Eliminates duplication between the ATF and FBI's separate explosives training facilities that are located in the same place, Redstone Arsenal in Huntsville, Alabama. **Savings: $4.625 mil-lion per year.**

➤ Rescinds $1 million from ATF's Violent Crime Reduction Pro-gram that the agency does not have the authority to spend and has unsuccessfully asked Congress to rescind on several previous occasions.

➢ Eliminates DEA's Mobile Enforcement Teams which, as the president stated, have "a narrow focus, are duplicative of other Federal, State, and local law enforcement efforts and their effectiveness in reducing crime has not been demonstrated." **Savings: $31 million per year.**

➢ Eliminates funding for the Juvenile Justice and Delinquency Prevention program, which is fraught with mismanagement, fraud, and duplication and is not a federal responsibility. In one egregious example of fraud, the DOJ Office of Inspector General found over $14,000 of grant funds were spent on food and beverage costs for 24 people for a 3-day conference in New Orleans, LA, which "exceeded allowable expenditures by $9620." **Savings: $280 million per year.**

DEPARTMENT OF LABOR – SAVINGS: $268.04 BILLION
Key points:

❖ Streamlines dozens of federal job training and employment programs so that states are empowered to serve the specific needs of their un- and under-employed populations.

❖ Strengthens program integrity of the Unemployment Insurance program.

❖ Refocuses the Occupational Safety and Health Administration's (OSHA) so it more efficiently spends taxpayer dollars while simultaneously enhancing worker safety.

❖ Terminates smaller programs that are duplicative, inefficient or outdated.

Recommendations & examples:

➢ Saves $11 million annually by terminating OSHA's Susan Harwood Grants, a program that is inefficient and duplicative of other federal efforts. For example, one grantee received nearly $200, 000 to develop and translate five training modules, and four years later American taxpayers received as a final product a 21 page PowerPoint presentation on "slips, trips, and falls," at a cost of $9,512 per slide.

➢ Ends unemployment benefits for the Bill Gates of the world. As many as 2,840 households who reported an income of $1 million or more on their tax returns were paid a total of $18.6 million in UI benefits in 2008, according to the Internal Revenue Service. This included more than 800 earning over $2 million and 17 with incomes exceeding $10 million. In all, multi-millionaires were paid $5.2 million in jobless benefits in 2008.[ii]

➢ Limits administrative dollars wasted by states administering the unemployment program. While basic office needs may be a reasonable expenditure, other expenditures are questionable. For example, Maine was recently found to have spent $60,000 of federal UI funds on a 36-foot mural containing images of labor unions strikes.[iii]

DEPARTMENT OF STATE AND FOREIGN AID – SAVINGS: $192.12 BILLION
Key points:

❖ Provides full funding to help vulnerable people around the world through spending on AIDS, malaria, child nutrition, and USAID's "Feed the Future" initiatives.

❖ Reduces foreign aid spending on countries that own billions of interest-paying US debt.

❖ Reduces programs for art and architecture exhibitions in Venice, Italy, education of foreign film directors, and music tours overseas.

❖ Maintains necessary spending for our allies and critical interests in the world.

DEPARTMENT OF TRANSPORTATION – SAVINGS: $192.22 BILLION
Key points:

❖ Enables the Highway Trust Fund to become solvent by reducing duplicative and low-priority highway spending through consolidation and elimination.

❖ Enables the Aviation and Airways Trust Fund to become solvent by reducing low-priority spending and limiting maximum appropriations from the trust fund to total no more than 90 percent of expected revenues.

❖ Streamlines and eliminates federal mandates that unnecessarily delay and even prevent needed transportation infrastructure projects and increase project costs.

❖ Further enables states, instead of Congress and the Administration, to prioritize critical highway and transit infrastructure improvements.

❖ Frees states to manage almost all of the federal gas taxes paid by its citizens if desired.

Recommendations & examples:

➢ Eliminates the requirement for states to spend around $600 million annually on bike paths, pedestrian walkways, highway beautification, and transportation museum projects, resulting in savings of $6 billion over ten years for taxpayers.

➢ Eliminates a program that uses highway dollars for historic covered bridge preservation projects to increase tourism in a select few states. Savings are $80 million over ten years.

➢ Eliminates a program that uses highway dollars for states to develop and maintain recreational trails and trail-related facilities. Savings are $850 million over ten years.

➢ Ends taxpayer support for subsidized food service on Amtrak. Savings are $850 million over ten years.

➢ Ends a $230 per month subsidy for federal employees' mass transit use that dramatically increased in costs as a result of a recent increase of $110 per month. Savings would total $4.32 billion over ten years.

DEPARTMENT OF VETERANS AFFAIRS – SAVINGS: $13.57 BILLION
Key points:

❖ Maintains full support for disabled veterans and education benefits for all combat veterans through the Post 9/11 GI Bill.

❖ Adopts common-sense recommendations for the VA to jointly purchase prescription drugs with the Department of Defense in order to reduce costs.

❖ Introduces cost-saving measures, such as copayments and annual fees, in VA health care for veterans well above the federal poverty line that are not injured or disabled from their military service.

U.S. ARMY OF CORPS OF ENGINEERS – SAVINGS: $5.28 BILLION
Key point:

❖ By eliminating low priority, parochial, and duplicative spending in the Corps of Engineers it will allow the agency to focus on meeting the nation's most urgent water infrastructure needs.

Recommendations:

➢ Terminate low-priority Corps construction projects –**savings: $2.3 billion**

➢ Eliminate water and wastewater treatment projects –**savings: $1.4 billion**

➢ End federal funding for beach replenishment projects –**savings: $702 million**

➢ Rescind $2 billion in unobligated balances – **savings: $500 million**

➢ Reducing excessive overhead costs and unnecessary bureaucracy —**savings: $2.66 million**

ENVIRONMENTAL PROTECTION AGENCY – SAVINGS: $33.67 BILLION
Key points:

❖ The core mission of the agency, to protect the environment and human health, is preserved by making common sense reductions to overlapping and inefficient programs.

❖ Spending on essential domestic environmental protection is prioritized over redundant international programs.

❖ Primary agency research programs will remain strong, while eliminating a secondary, poorly focused research grant program.

❖ President Obama's recommendations for administrative efficiency and lower overhead are adopted, ensuring greater efficiency.

Recommendations & examples:

➢ Reins in EPA multi-million dollar conference travel that has resulted in trips to vacation hotspots, including a dinner cruises on the River Seine in Paris. **Savings: $25 million over next five years.**

➢ Ends a program in which only one state, California, qualifies, and another program in which only one state, California, receives the majority of funds. This will ensure that all states are treated equitably and fairly. **Savings: $200 million.**

➢ Terminates a duplicative and unnecessary outside research program that has funded extraneous items like research into "sustainable" fashion and apparel, including shoes made of chicken feathers, flaxseed and soybean oil, and a smart-lock for shared bicycles. **Savings: $600 million.**

NASA - SAVINGS: $51.15 BILLION
Key points:

❖ NASA is refocused on space exploration, including the eventual return of a U.S. manned space program, by eliminating unrelated and duplicative programs distracting the agency from its core missions.

Recommendations & examples:

➤ Because the United States no longer has a manned space program, NASA will pay $56 million per seat to send astronauts on voyages aboard Russian spaceships.

➤ Only a third of NASA's budget is spent for space operations and aeronautics.

➤ NASA researchers are working to improve the quality of California wines and helped developed the swimsuit worn by Michael Phelps at the 2008 Summer Olympics.

➤ NASA projects are notoriously over budget, behind, schedule, or both, and just nine projects account for cost overruns in excess of $1.2 billion.

➤ The NASA Inspector General has failed to prevent or identify waste, saving only 36 cents for every dollar spent compared to an average of $9.49 saved per dollar spent by the IGs of other agencies.

NATIONAL SCIENCE FOUNDATION – SAVINGS: $14.20 BILLION
Key point:

❖ By prioritizing NSF's funding on transformative scientific research it will ensure we can retain America's scientific edge without adding to the debt threatening the economic engines that power our nation's leadership role in the world.

Recommendations & examples:

➢ Eliminate NSF's Social, Behavioral and Economics (SBE) Directorate – **savings: $2.8 billion**

➢ Rescind unspent, expired funds NSF currently holds – **savings: $1.7 billion**

SMALL BUSINESS ADMINISTRATION – SAVINGS: $3.22 BILLION
Key points:

❖ Under current standards, the SBA typically defines a "small business" as those with less than $7 million in revenues and fewer than 500 employees. The definition is so broad, however, that it encompass 99.7 percent of all U.S. businesses. As a result, regular claims are made, by no less than GAO and the agency's own inspector general, that large businesses are abusing the programs to the exclusion of small ones.

❖ Improper payment problems – ex) the inspector general reports that improper payments for the 7(a) business loan program were 27 percent in 2009, while they were 46 percent for disaster loans. Combined, this represented more than $2.3 billion in government loans.

❖ The need for small business loan guarantee programs has diminished greatly in recent years. First, the 7(a) program is intended for creditworthy borrowers, but billions of dollars in losses since 2008 demonstrate that the agency has a poor track record in administering taxpayer dollars for this purpose. Second, there was more than $609 billion in outstanding small business loans during the first quarter of 2011.

PRESERVING SOCIAL SECURITY FOR FUTURE GENERATIONS SOCIAL SECURITY & SOCIAL– 75 YEAR SOLVENCY
Key points:

❖ Places Social Security, with its current $6.5 trillion unfunded obligation, on a solvent path over the 75-year window – eliminating the program's current 2.22 percent actuarial deficit.

❖ Helps fulfill the mission of Social Security to combat poverty-ridden old age by modernizing the program, strengthening work incentives, enriching benefits for lower income earners dependent on the system, and slowing benefit growth of workers who can afford to save more for retirement on their own – and without increasing taxes.

❖ Modernizes the Social Security disability programs and strengthens safeguards to deter waste, fraud and abuse.

❖ Refocuses the Social Security Administration's current culture of solely paying benefits to balancing the equally important responsibilities of managing entitlements and performing program integrity.

❖ Saves $17 billion over 10 years in the SSI program.

Recommendations:

➢ Alters the retirement age to reflect life expectancy. This Normal Retirement Age (NRA) would *gradually increase* – one month every two years. This means individuals who turn age 62 in 2046 will have a NRA of 68, and those who turn age 62 in 2070 will have an NRA of 69. The Earliest Eligibility Age would also gradually increase in tandem with the Normal Retirement Age.

➢ Switches to a more accurate measure of inflation for Social Security cost-of-living-adjustments (COLAs) by using "chained-CPI" to measure inflation.

➢ Alters the progressive benefit formula of current law, slowing benefit growth, especially for higher earners. Under the changes in the benefit formula, benefits are enriched so that workers below the 40th percentile are "held harmless" from changes and experience a slight benefit increase under the formula. Above the 40th percentile, benefit growth is restrained by lowering the amount the current system replaces.

➢ Alters the spousal benefit to better reflect costs of a two-person household, while also strengthening the connection between taxes paid and benefits received.

➢ Modernizes the Social Security disability programs and strengthens safeguards to deter waste, fraud and abuse.

Social Security Disability Insurance:
Key points:

❖ Encourages a shift in the culture of SSA from solely paying benefits to a strong balance between the equally important responsibilities of managing the disability programs and enforcing program rules through program integrity functions.

❖ Updates the disability application and appellate process to ensure only the truly disabled that cannot work any job in the national economy are accepted into the program and able Americans are encouraged to be productive and return to work.

❖ Encourages state involvement in helping adults on SSI find gainful employment and children on SSI receive the educational help they need to grow into independent adults.

REVENUE
TAX EXPENDITURES
Key point:

❖ Immediately ends dozens of special interest giveaways and eliminates spending through tax code, which will generate revenue, but without increasing tax rates.

Examples:

➢ Ends tax breaks for Hollywood movie producers. Savings: $1,000,000,000
➢ Eliminate IRS Tax Exemptions for Bailout Recipients

Savings:

➢ Reform tax expenditures. Savings: **$962.02 billion**
➢ Other government revenue. Savings: **$30.34 billion**

TOTAL: $9.032 TRILLION

Appendix C—Federal Code Titles

Title 1 - General Provisions

Title 2 - Grants and Agreements

Title 3 - The President

Title 4 - Accounts

Title 5 - Administrative Personnel

Title 6 - Domestic Security

Title 7 - Agriculture

Title 8 - Aliens and Nationality

Title 9 - Animals and Animal Products

Title 10 - Energy

Title 11 - Federal Elections

Title 12 - Banks and Banking

Title 13 - Business Credit and Assistance

Title 14 - Aeronautics and Space

Title 15 - Commerce and Foreign Trade

Title 16 - Commercial Practices

Title 17 - Commodity and Securities Exchanges

Title 18 - Conservation of Power and Water Resources

Title 19 - Customs Duties

Title 20 - Employees' Benefits

Title 21 - Food and Drugs

Title 22 - Foreign Relations

Title 23 - Highways

Title 24 - Housing and Urban Development

Title 25 - Indians

Title 26 - Internal Revenue

Title 27 - Alcohol, Tobacco Products and Firearms

Title 28 - Judicial Administration

Title 29 - Labor

Title 30 - Mineral Resources

Title 31 - Money and Finance: Treasury

Title 32 - National Defense

Title 33 - Navigation and Navigable Waters

Title 34 - Education

Title 35 - Panama Canal

Title 36 - Parks, Forests, and Public Property

Title 37 - Patents, Trademarks, and Copyrights

Title 38 - Pensions, Bonuses, and Veterans' Relief

Title 39 - Postal Service

Title 40 - Protection of Environment

Title 41 - Public Contracts and Property Management

Title 42 - Public Health

Title 43 - Public Lands: Interior

Title 44 - Emergency Management and Assistance

Title 45 - Public Welfare

Title 46 - Shipping

Title 47 - Telecommunication

Title 48 - Federal Acquisition Regulations System

Title 49 - Transportation

Title 50 - Wildlife and Fisheries

Endnotes

1   Saul Alinsky, *Rules for Radicals*

2   *Human Events* http://www.humanevents.com/article. php?id=45037

3   survey by McKinsey & Company http://www.mckinsey-quarterly.com/How_US_health_care_reform_will_affect_ employee_benefits_2813

4   Institute for Energy Research http://www.instituteforener-gyresearch.org/2012/02/23/ier-analysis-oil-and-gas-produc-tion-declines-on-federal-lands-in-fy2011/

5   IER reports http://www.instituteforenergyresearch. org/2012/03/13/exposing-the-2-percent-oil-reserves-myth/

6   Heritage Foundation Study http://www.heritage.org/ research/reports/2012/03/red-tape-rising-obama-era-regula-tion-at-the-three-year-mark

7   Wall Street Journal article http://online.wsj.com/article/ SB10000872396390443792604577574910276629448. html?mod=opinion_newsreel

8   2011 the debt http://www.usgovernmentspending.com/ year2011_0.html

9   Growth In The Time Of Debt http://www.economics.har-vard.edu/files/faculty/51_Growth_in_Time_Debt_aer.pdf

10   Government Report http://www.pri.org/stories/politics-soci-ety/government/as-unemployment-benefits-claims-decline-disability-claims-rise-7705.html

11   study by the Laffer Center http://www.laffercenter.com/2011/04/the-economic-burden-caused-by-tax-code-complexity/

12   2011 study http://mpra.ub.uni-muenchen.de/29672/1/MPRA_paper_29672.pdf

13   Tax Foundation Special Report http://www.taxfoundation.org/files/sr138.pdf

14   report by Freedom Works http://www.freedomworks.org/scrapthecode/topten.php

15   General Accounting Office (GAO) published reports http://www.gao.gov/assets/590/588818.pdf

16   written testimony http://www.coburn.senate.gov/public/index.cfm?a=Files.Serve&File_id=ed30e791-037c-45c6-aa7b-62f3a52b781a

17   Institute for Energy Research http://www.instituteforener-gyresearch.org/2012/01/12/government-forces-refiners-to-pay-fine-for-nonexistent-ethanol/

18   An Annual Snapshot of the Federal Regulatory State http://cei.org/sites/default/files/Wayne%20Crews%20-%2010,000%20Commandments%202011.pdf

19 Heritage Foundation Report http://www.heritage.org/
    research/reports/2012/03/red-tape-rising-obama-era-regula-
    tion-at-the-three-year-mark

20 SBA study http://archive.sba.gov/advo/research/rs371tot.pdf

21 *Updated Estimates for the Insurance Coverage Provisions of
    the Affordable Care Act* http://www.cbo.gov/sites/default/
    files/cbofiles/attachments/03-13-Coverage%20Estimates.pdf

22 November 30, 2010 Congressional Research Services Report.
    http://epw.senate.gov/public/index.cfm?FuseAction=Files.
    view&FileStore_id=04212e22-c1b3-41f2-b0ba-0da5eaead952

23 U.S. oil resources: President Obama's 'non sequitur facts'
    http://www.washingtonpost.com/blogs/fact-checker/
    post/us-oil-resources-president-obamas-non-sequitur-
    facts/2012/03/14/glQApP14CS_blog.html

24 Rand said in a report http://www.rand.org/pubs/mono-
    graphs/2005/RAND_MG414.pdf

25 Institute for Energy Research http://www.instituteforener-
    gyresearch.org/2012/02/23/ier-analysis-oil-and-gas-produc-
    tion-declines-on-federal-lands-in-fy2011/

26 US Energy Information Administration http://www.eia.gov/
    analysis/requests/subsidy/

27 Heritage Foundation http://blog.heritage.org/2012/02/21/
    morning-bell-buying-house-votes-for-unpopular-legislation/

28 Saul Alinsky, Rules for Radicals

29 Paul Kengor Ph.D., *The Communist*

30   http://www.nationalreview.com/articles/224610/inside-obamas-acorn/stanley-kurtz?pg=1

31   David Horowitz, *Barack Obama's Rules for Revolution the Alinsky Model*

32   *The Path to Prosperity* http://budget.house.gov/Uploaded-Files/Pathtoprosperity2013.pdf

www.ingramcontent.com/pod-product-compliance
Lightning Source LLC
Chambersburg PA
CBHW070000300526
45794CB00001B/127